OUR LIVING LANGUAGE
a guide to effective Speech Communication

by
Gillian Cohen
FLCM, LLCM(TD), ALCM

LCM Publications

First published in 1998
By LCN Publications
Thames Valley University
St Mary's Road
London W5 5RF

Printed in England by
Basingstoke Press Ltd
Wade Road
Basingstoke
Hants RG24 8QW

© Gillian Cohen 1997

All rights reserved. No part of this publication may be reproduced, stored in a retrieval system or transmitted in any form or by means, electronic, mechanical, photocopying, recording or otherwise, without prior permission in writing of the copyright owner.

ISBN 0-9528375-2-8

CONTENTS

	PAGE
Acknowledgements	
Foreword	1
Why do we need technique?	
In support of the theory of speech.	
Introduction	5
Language - our most effective means of communication.	
Grade 1	10
Introducing the new alphabet of sounds - starting with vowels - instruments of expression.	
Grade 2	18
Consonants - provide the framework of our words.	
Grade 3	27
The nature of word grouping - developing a sensitivity towards language.	
Grade 4	35
Breathing for Speech and Drama - why do we need to develop a method?	
Grade 5	56
Speech colour - enhancing the words we use.	
Grade 6	75
Modulation - using the elements of vocal variety to communicate text.	
Formation of vowel and consonant sounds.	
Grade 7	115
Verse Pauses.	
Rhythm and Metre in Prose & Verse.	
Common Speech Faults and their correction.	
Grade 8	145
Voice Production - breathing, projection, resonance and modulation.	
Conclusion	158
Performance - how our technique underpins successful communication.	
Index	161
Sources Consulted	

ACKNOWLEDGEMENTS

The author would like to express her thanks to the following people for their help in preparing this book:

>Dr Kenneth Pickering
>Gillian Patch
>Leena Arjoon
>Dr J Maxwell Hargreaves

With special thanks to my wonderful and supportive family and especially my husband, Stephen.

For permission to publish extracts from poems and prose in this book, acknowledgement is made to the following:

- For *The Twits* by Roald Dahl, published by Cape.
- For *The Wind in the Willows* by Kenneth Grahame, copyright, The University Chest, Oxford, reproduced by permission of Curtis Brown, London.
- For 'Moods of Rain' by Vernon Scannell from *New and Collected Poems 1950-1993*, published by Robson Books Ltd.
- For *The Birds* by Daphne du Maurier, reproduced with permission of Curtis Brown Ltd, London on behalf of The Chichester Partnership. Copyright 1952, Daphne du Maurier Browning.
- For *Conversation Piece* by Gareth Owen, copyright Gareth Owen 1988, Scholastic Collections.
- For *Lord of the Flies* by William Golding, published by Faber & Faber.
- For 'Piano' by DH Lawrence from *The Complete Poems of DH Lawrence*. Acknowledgement is made to Lawrence Pollinger Limited and the Estate of Freida Lawrence Ravagli.

FOREWORD

This book has been written especially for students and teachers preparing for the examinations in Speech, Drama and Communication of the London College of Music.

However, it will, in fact, benefit any student studying and pursuing an interest in Speech, Drama and Communication and taking the public examinations of other examining boards.

This informal but informative guide aims to demonstrate how important it is to *apply* the theory to the practical work and to re-establish the value of theory as a basis for effective communication. Anyone can digest information and learn definitions but the real test is applying our knowledge - and this requires a thorough understanding.

We explain clearly what is expected from our candidates at each grade. A wealth of material abounds and we felt there was a need for easier access to this information. We have carefully considered what our students need to know at each stage and why: a sufficient amount to guide students to develop a better performance or presentation, which is our ultimate aim. The question which should remain uppermost in our minds is "why do we need to learn / teach this?". There is also a need to justify why we, as a Board, have traditionally placed so much emphasis on learning, understanding and applying Theory to practical work. Practical use of the theory will lead to a greater understanding of a text and assist in assembling our thoughts into words.

'My words fly up, my thoughts remain below, words without thoughts never to heaven go.'
Hamlet

Foreword

Please note that from Grade 2 onwards, candidates may be asked questions from previous grades. This, in fact, reinforces our belief that the theory needs to be constantly revised. As questions will be related to the candidate's practical work wherever possible, the study of theory therefore assumes some relevance. This underlines how important it is that the theory is no longer seen as a separate element of the examination. Candidates entering the examination system at higher grades should therefore make sure that the theory requirements of the earlier grades are covered.

There is a logical sequence of cumulative knowledge throughout the Speech and Drama Grades. We feel it is important that teachers should encourage all their students to study the theory Guidelines as a working manual - and not just for the particular examinations where the Theory is actually discussed. The study of technique helps create a better performance - as the theory of speech explains the mechanics of our craft: relaxation, effective breathing, phrasing, tone, projection and articulation. Through familiarity and practice these should become second nature, allowing us to concentrate and focus on the intention of what we wish to communicate. As with any new skill we adopt, conscious behaviour will eventually become subconscious. Mastery of Technique is 'the Art that Conceals Art'. Well-absorbed technique opens our minds to further possibilities allowing us to enjoy communicating and responding to our audience. Theory and performance are inter-related: one highlights the other. Our manual guides our students into developing an extra dimension to their work.

Our examinations exist to help each individual release his or her own creative potential, whether in teaching, at the workplace or in the theatre. Our aim is clear, expressive, natural speech, full of energy and vitality. All our examinations are concerned with the Spoken Word. In our syllabus we either interpret and perform the words of a writer or assemble our own thoughts into words. We need to focus on the significance of words and their associations and communicate their emotional content.

Foreword

Students learn to become aware of the structure of language and how we need to choose words appropriately. Lucid speaking takes time and practice - the study of technique develops an appreciation of the impact of words, as we connect to the sounds of words.

> *'Language is the dress of thought.'*
> **Samuel Johnson**

Writers can make us all more aware of the huge and expressive vocabulary in our English Language. The ideas and the images conveyed by imaginative writing influence our own choice of words. We develop the confidence to explore and expand our language. Enjoying the words and thought-patterns of a writer helps develop our own expressiveness.

Communication is the means whereby we convey information - in words or in gestures, facial expression, movement (our body language), and how we succeed in conveying this effectively. Our imagination provokes our thoughts and ideas into words. Effective delivery is achieved by confident, clear, concise, expressive and appropriate language. We need to develop our ability to use vivid speech, develop fluency and a vitality to our speech and to appreciate the musicality of words. Our voices are an expression of our personalities - and we have the power of expressing and sharing our thoughts.

Through well-absorbed technique we communicate mood, emotion, dynamism - that vital spark needed in performance. From understanding comes that feeling of inner confidence, of being in control - we then have the freedom to be creative and allow our audience to relax and 'suspend disbelief' during our performances. Confidence comes from thorough preparation and secure technique - these eliminate fear and anxiety and create a sense of individuality and allow us to release the untapped potential within us!

Foreword

All our technical expertise should make our performances seem effortless - we create an illusion of spontaneity. Words mustn't be delivered as mere words - we need concentration to re-create the situation and the thoughts afresh. Remember what you first noticed about your pieces - your first impressions - so that performances are convincing and never stale. Our basic human need to communicate is realised through energy and personal magnetism - that vital, dynamic spark of life we aim to develop.

INTRODUCTION

From our Introductory Exams - the Steps - up to Grade Five we ask about *the meaning of the pieces performed and the vocabulary in the pieces.* What is our purpose behind these questions?

We use *words* as a means of communication and language is our most effective form of communication. Words came about because of the *physical need* to express a situation. We learn to speak by imitation. Speech patterns are formed in childhood - notice how families tend to sound alike! - the same stress patterns on words, the same accent, the same choice of words. Speaking is something most of us do automatically, every day of our lives, without a great deal of conscious thought. Speech Training *awakens* imaginative awareness as we explore the impact and power of the Spoken Word. We learn to re-connect the thought with the word.

> *'He gave man speech, and speech created thought, which is the measure of the Universe.'*
> **Shelley**

We need to re-discover the meanings of words and their associations - to explore our language and re-connect to the sounds contained in words. During our formative years, when the pattern of language is usually established, we delighted in discovering new words, their sounds and associations and the pleasure we felt in sharing them.

Many of us have lost our *sensitivity* for listening and responding to sounds, and in modern times, largely through the influence of television, we have lost many of our oral traditions such as reading out aloud and storytelling. Our aim is to let words stimulate and free our imaginations. We learn to become aware of the impact of speech sounds and the images words evoke. *Sound* is the basis of our imagination.

Introduction

Candidates are asked about: *the meaning of pieces performed and the vocabulary in the pieces.* By asking about meanings of pieces and individual words - we are making sure that candidates have a thorough knowledge of their pieces and that there has been thought and understanding applied to their work. Our candidates are made to consider the effect words and their associations have on the imagination enabling them to re-create work as the writer intended. We help candidates develop their listening skills, *listening* as opposed to hearing. 'Listening' suggests *concentration* and *thought*. How many familiar sounds do we hear but inadvertently ignore in our daily lives? Many candidates have learnt to read fluently, and words are pronounced correctly, but they have no real understanding of their meanings. Speech training is 'ear training' and sound becomes sight with vivid 'word painting'. We need to listen before we can react and respond. We need to ask ourselves 'is our performance accurate to our intentions?' Our voice is the means by which we communicate our inner self. Is it accurate to the writer's intentions? ..to the piece we are interpreting? ..to the writer's inner voice? Words paint a verbal picture - have we succeeded in colouring words, focusing on the light and shade, capturing the style of the piece?

In our examinations we start to explore the impact of descriptive words - we learn how writers use *onomatopoeia*, *alliteration* and *assonance* for effect and in turn how much more expressive our speech becomes. We need to develop the skill of speaking the words out aloud - there is a huge difference between reading to oneself and sharing words out aloud - and own-choice pieces should be selected accordingly! We need to take more care over responding to phrasing, to the writer's thought-pattern, to punctuation, using the pause points. Study how pieces are constructed - length of phrases, choice of words. Think about the opening and ending of your pieces; why do they make an impact?

For example in **Onomatopoeia** - the sounds in the word resemble the meaning associated with it - 'sizzle, splash, buzz, howl, crash, whisper.'

Introduction

In **Alliteration** - the same consonant sound repeated at the beginning of words is used to great effect by writers - 'cool, calm and collected'...' forest's ferny floor' - to create mood and atmosphere.

In **Assonance** - the repetition of vowel sounds in adjoining words. The pattern of sound helps to create the tone of the piece because repeated sounds impress themselves upon the mind, and can be very effective - smooth, cool, pool.

(Please note - candidates are *not* expected to define the technical terms above at the early grades, but need to be made aware of the devices writers use, so that they are able to appreciate their qualities.)

These devices allow the performer to communicate more effectively with appropriate expression. Listen to the effect words have on the ears - slush, smooth, dirty, shiver, plunge, snap - a combination of expressive vowel and consonant sounds, emphasised by short or long vowel sounds and descriptive consonants. Enjoy experimenting with these sounds to get the effects you want. Think about these words: 'groan' 'grumble' 'delicious'. We are developing our ability to think and concentrate and enjoy the spoken word. In music we learn about 'dynamics' - the varying degree of volume of sounds - we also have ' verbal dynamics' - the musicality of words, which trigger our sensory awareness.

In Grades 1 and 2 we will learn about vowel and consonants sounds in some depth - these are the components of our language and speech. We draw attention to the new alphabet of sounds; vowels are the instruments of *expression* in any word, they provide the 'tone' in our voice. The consonants provide the structure and framework of words and we aim to explore the impact that certain consonants can have. Individual sounds connect to make words. Words have muscular *energy* - this energy is released through the force of our breath flow and the efficiency of our speech organs, controlled of course by the need and desire to share words. It is this muscular energy in

Introduction

words that allows us to take the volume down and still be heard. 'Voice' is not a separate entity to be studied in isolation, it is part of our whole being: - our mood, our state of mind, our aspirations, our success and failures are all reflected in our tone of voice and the willingness to communicate. For example, when people mumble, do we assume it is a reluctance to communicate through a lack of confidence, a feeling that they are not worth listening to, or just a bad habit they've adopted? Speech Training explores all these issues.

As all our examinations cover some aspect of the spoken word, our aim is to help candidates put more *expression* into words and to enjoy sharing them; to develop and strengthen their choice of vocabulary and to bring out the colour and significance of words and their associations. Words take on different meanings depending on their context. Be aware of the subtle nuances words can reveal.

Finally, how do we create a feeling of *spontaneity* in a performance? Too many pieces presented at examinations appear over-worked, stale and lacking in energy. We need an immediate response to words - and to be able to remember that initial response, always re-creating the thought and situation afresh at each repetition. This develops our skill of concentration so that the performance does not become mechanical.

Learn to react to words in sight readings - e.g. 'whisper', 'bellow', 'sneak' - or evocative lines such as - 'whenever the trees are crying aloud'. Give these words their full value and aim to breathe some life, some emotion, directly and instantaneously into these images. Words create mood and atmosphere and we learn to empathise with them. 'Suddenly our eyes are opened to the possibilities ....'

'Words are but the signs of ideas.'
Samuel Johnson

Introduction

To summarise the main points

- Explore the meanings of words and their associations.

- Discover *sound* values in words - these add an extra dimension to your work.

- Create a verbal picture with words, through the instrument of voice, coupled with facial expressions, gestures and body language.

- Share your work - aim for vivid, effective speech, appropriate to the content of your pieces.

- Our examinations inspire candidates to *think* and to create an illusion of spontaneity in their work.

GRADE ONE

Candidates are asked about:
- **The recognition of a vowel sound**
- **The differences between single and double vowels**

We speak with sounds, individual sounds which connect to make words. We call these sounds, vowels and consonants. We use the letters of the alphabet for spelling and writing - there are 5 vowel sounds we use when learning to read and write:

a, e, i, o, u - whereas in speech there are 25 vowel sounds!

For Grade 1 we are going to learn about the 12 *single vowel* sounds and the 8 *double vowel* sounds. The other 5 vowel sounds (triphthongs) are discussed in Grade 6.

What actually is a vowel sound?

Let me first explain briefly how we make and hear a sound. We need two elements, something that strikes and something that is struck and which resists the impact, to a greater or lesser degree, and vibrates accordingly.

These vibrations disturb the surrounding air and set up sound waves which we receive through our ears. With voice, the breath is the initial impulse which strikes against the vocal cords in the voice box (larynx). The edges of the vocal cords come together (approximate) when you want to make sound and the breath force causes them to vibrate.

These vibrations set up sound waves which can then be 'resonated' - which means that the sound reverberates (and is amplified) in the cavities of the chest, throat, mouth, nose and head. We depend on the breath to start the sound, but it is *the way we use the breath* to strike the cords before it enters the resonating cavities, that we hear differences of tone (harsh or

Grade 1

breathy). Although we all make the sound in the *same way*, we are all different shapes and sizes and we can change the size and shape of the main resonator, the mouth, with the movement of the jaw, the lips, tongue and soft palate.

It is important to understand how sound is made and where breath is made into sound, though this information will *not* be asked for by the examiner. This overall picture gives us a greater understanding of breath and voice and enables us now to explain specifically how we make a *vowel* sound.

A vowel sound is produced in the voice box (larynx) by the breath flow vibrating on the vocal cords - vowels are always vocalised, (i.e. a sound made with the voice). Incidentally, there is only a slight buzz heard from the vocal cords. ***The sound we hear is largely formed by the shaping of our lips and the position of the tongue and jaw. There is a free flow of breath through the mouth and the sound is spoken through a freely open mouth - this is how we can recognise a vowel sound. The sound is not interrupted by any of our speech organs, which are:- the tongue, teeth, lips, and the hard and soft palate.*** The tongue, lips and soft palate are muscular. Think of the hard palate as a sounding board - the hard gum ridge behind your top front teeth; many of our English speech sounds are formed here and it is a very important part of your mouth to explore.

Our tongue tip is held down behind the front bottom teeth when speaking vowel sounds in isolation. Usually when speaking, we are always moving from or to a consonant - (say the words 'late' and 'father' in slow motion and think about the positions of your tongue as you say the word).

A **single vowel** is one complete and unaltered sound, which means the shape does not alter as we say it. Notice how some sounds are made predominantly by the shape of our lips and some by the position of our tongue, which we categorise as lip vowels / tongue vowels. We have short-sounding single vowels and long-sounding single vowels, which means that the sound is

Grade 1

either finished quickly (a short sound) or the sound can be sustained for as long as we have enough breath (therefore we can make a longer sound)!

The length of short or long vowels actually varies according to the consonants that follow - think about these words and experiment with the effect you wish to create - r<u>i</u>p, sn<u>a</u>p, sm<u>oo</u>th, c<u>oo</u>l. Now compare - pr<u>e</u>ss, p<u>u</u>ll, pl<u>u</u>nge. Do you notice how some consonants take longer to say than others - and how you automatically lengthen the vowel sound to help colour the word?

There are 7 short single vowels and the easiest way to remember them is to learn the following sentence:

Th<u>a</u>t b<u>oo</u>k <u>i</u>s n<u>o</u>t m<u>u</u>ch b<u>e</u>tt<u>e</u>r.

(We call this a mnemonic - which is a device used to help you remember something else!)

It is much easier to learn a sentence containing the sounds in words, than trying to remember a list of the 20 vowel sounds needed for Grade 1. We are also made aware of the vowel sounds in words as opposed to hearing them in isolation. We learn to *listen* for the sounds instead of looking at the spelling. Vowels can be written in different ways, but make the same sound. For example, the sound 'ee' can be written; th<u>e</u>se, ch<u>ee</u>se, br<u>ea</u>the, thi<u>e</u>f, c<u>ei</u>ling, and mach<u>i</u>ne! You need to be able to recognise and demonstrate this to the examiner; examples therefore are important and you should be able to identify some more examples of vowels from your own words. Make sure you are able to separate the examples of the vowel sounds in the words for the examiner - don't just repeat the learnt sentence or the whole word! *The sounds are underlined.*

Practice saying the vowel sounds out aloud, think about the positions of the jaw and lip shapes and keep the tongue tip held down behind the bottom front teeth - use a mirror to see the different movements. Make sure you have a thumb-width

Grade 1

opening of your mouth - if you don't open your mouths, you'll trap the sound in! Now say oo-ee-ah - we go from a small lip opening, to a neutral lip shape, to a wide opening!

The 5 single long-sounding vowels are heard in:

We do far more work!

Double vowels are vowel sounds formed by two single vowels joined together, spoken without interruption. The sounds flow into each other and are said in the same space of time as one single sound vowel. (My own pupils have always been curious to know which two single vowels make up our double vowels and so I list them *below* for your interest - though you will *not* be asked to identify these by the examiner. If the single vowels are spoken in slow motion - to exaggerate which two vowels glide together, you will be aware that we make TWO SHAPES with our mouths! The first vowel in the double vowel sound is emphasised more strongly than the second.

There are 8 double vowels altogether - 5 'falling' and 3 'centring'. Compare the movement of your mouth between the two categories.

With the 'falling' double vowels the length and stress *falls* from the *first* vowel and onto the second vowel sound. The 5 'falling' double vowels are contained in the following sentence:

Mice don't make loud noises.

a) **Mice** - 'i' in 'mice' is made up of the vowel sounds in 'had' and 'hid'.
b) **don't** - 'oh' in 'don't' is made up of the vowel sounds in 'the' and 'put'.
c) **make** - 'ay' in 'make' is made up of the vowel sounds in the words 'pet' and 'pit'.
d) **loud** - 'ow' in 'loud' is made up of the vowel sounds in 'had' and 'put'.

Grade 1

e) n**oi**ses - 'oy' in 'noises' is made up of the vowel sounds in 's<u>aw</u>' and 'h<u>i</u>d'.

With the *'centring'* double vowels the main stress is on the *first* vowel sound which *glides into* the second sound - but onto the neutral vowel - (which is the shortest vowel sound and is always placed in an unaccented position), and therefore the movement is marginal.

The 3 *'centring'* double vowels end in the neutral vowel sound (the sound contained in the word th<u>e</u>) - p<u>ie</u>r, p<u>ai</u>r, p<u>oo</u>r.

a) *p**ie**r* - is made up of the vowel sounds in 'p<u>i</u>t' and 'th<u>e</u>'.
b) *p**ai**r* - is made up of the vowel sounds in 'p<u>e</u>t and 'th<u>e</u>'.
c) *p**oo**r* - is made up of the vowel sounds in 'p<u>u</u>t' and 'th<u>e</u>'.

You may be interested to know which vowel sounds are made predominately by the lips (the shape of the lips varies from a closed circle to an open mouth) and those classed as tongue vowels, defined by the position of the tongue (where it goes from a flat position to a very arched one). You will *not* be asked for this information by the examiner - but as we are exploring how vowel sounds are made, we thought you would enjoy discovering these differences!

With the lip vowels, the lip shapes dominate (minimal tongue movement); with the tongue vowels the tongue position governs (neutral lips).

The following are *single vowel* sounds shaped by the *lips*:

OO	as in ch<u>oo</u>se	long sound
oo	as in b<u>oo</u>k	short sound
AW	as in s<u>aw</u>	long sound
o	as in sh<u>o</u>t	short sound

Notice how the lips change shape from a small round opening through to a wide open mouth, and relaxed jaw! Keep the tongue tip down behind the bottom front teeth. Make sure your teeth aren't clenched! It is much easier to look at the shapes

Grade 1

The *tongue* single vowels are as follows :-

AH	as in m<u>a</u>rk	long sound
u	as in l<u>u</u>nch	short sound
ER	as in l<u>ea</u>rn	long sound
er (neutral)	as in fath<u>er</u>	short sound
a	as in c<u>a</u>t	short sound
e	as in b<u>e</u>d	short sound
i	as in th<u>i</u>nk	short sound
EE	as in s<u>ee</u>	long sound

The tongue is flat in AH - changing position so that by the time you get to EE - the tongue is very arched in front.

The *double vowel* sounds, made primarily by the *lips* are:

OH	as in g<u>o</u>
OW	as in h<u>ou</u>se
OI	as in b<u>oy</u>

The *double vowel* sounds, made primarily by the *tongue* are:

AY	as in d<u>ay</u>
I	as in sk<u>y</u>
EAR	as in p<u>ier</u>
AIR	as in h<u>air</u>
OOR	as in p<u>oor</u>

For a more detailed classification, please refer to the vowel chart in Chapter 6.

When saying these sounds, think also about throwing the sounds forward. This gives the optimum resonance to each sound! Consider how we metaphorically throw sounds and words forward out of our mouths when we want to communicate! Then there is a willingness to share thoughts and ideas, display feelings. More energy is released.

Grade 1

Experiment with keeping the sound in the back of the throat and hear the difference. Tense the lips, stretch them back. Clench the teeth and jaw. What does it do to the sound - can you hear and feel the difference?

You are developing sensory awareness to give sounds their full value. We are developing our listening skills; *speech* work trains the *ear*. TV advertising uses this knowledge to its advantage - listen to the words used to sell a product - cool ice cream, smooth chocolate.

> *'Hoover beats as it sweeps as it cleans.'*
> *'Drinka Pinta Milka Day.'*
> *'More Cheese please Louise.'*
> *'Savour the Flavour.'*

These advertising slogans use the repetition of vowel sounds - Assonance - repeated sounds impress themselves upon the mind and can be very effective. Vowel sounds convey 'emotion' - the tone of our voices - which we interpret as sounding happy, cross, despondent, sad.

You may think there is a lot of teaching material here for such an early stage - Grade One - but as candidates are being introduced to so many new ideas - sound, *vowel sounds* as opposed to *symbols used in writing*, identifying their speech organs - what they are and how we use them, it is important to have an explanation and understanding of the overall picture. This does influence the quality of a candidate's work, and it is no coincidence that we find that a thorough understanding of the theory is coupled with imaginative performances.

Grade 1

To summarise the main points

- In speech we think about sounds in words not the spelling.

- We recognise a vowel sound because the sound comes out uninterrupted. There is a free passage of sound through the mouth but it is shaped in different ways, for the differing sounds.

- A single vowel is one complete and unaltered sound. Some sounds are finished quickly, others are longer sounding.

- Learn the mnemonics - the sentences are very useful as an aid to learning - much better than a long list.

- Double vowels consist of two single vowels - the first gliding into the second - therefore our mouths make two shapes - made in the same space of time as one single long-sounding vowel.

- The sound we hear is formed by the shaping of our lips and the position of the tongue. A relaxed jaw is important. Always aim to throw the sound forward, tongue tip down.

- You are developing your sensory awareness to give sounds their full value - we start in Grade One with the vowels - these sounds convey the tone of our voices - vowels are the instruments of expression in any word, therefore a very good starting point for our work!

GRADE TWO

Candidates are asked about:
- **The recognition of a consonant sound.**
- **The meaning of the terms 'voiced and unvoiced', 'sustained and plosive'.**

In Grade One we discovered how sound is made - we learnt that a vowel sound is spoken through a freely open mouth and jaw. The breath vibrates on the vocal cords (all vowel sounds are vocalised/voiced ie. a sound made with the voice). There is a free flow of breath through the mouth - and the sound is made by the shaping of the lips and position of the tongue.

Now in Grade Two we shall explain about consonant sounds - we have 21 consonant letters in the alphabet but 24 different consonant sounds in speech.

We need to define a consonant sound:- here the passage of air is stopped or partially interrupted by one or more organs of speech, which are: the tongue, teeth, lips, hard and soft palate. Therefore the sound does not come out immediately (as in a vowel sound). We can change the shape of the mouth with the movement of the jaw - and learn to use the muscles of the lips, tongue and soft palate to their full advantage. The hard palate is used as a sounding board.

Consonants are either termed *voiced* (vocalised) or *unvoiced* (aspirate):

- **Voiced (or vocal) consonants** are made by the breath vibrating on the vocal cords - that is to say the vocal cords come together ('approximate') when you say them and so they are sounded or vibrated. These sounds are important because of the possible vibrations that could be made, thereby adding an extra dimension to the sound. Put your

Grade 2

hand on your voice box and feel the vibration.

e.g. **b** as in bed   **d** as in dog   **v** as in voice
   z as in zoo   **g** as in get   **w** as in we
   m as in man   **n** as in no   **ng** as in ring
   l as in leg   **r** as in red   **j** as in jar
   th as in this   **zh** as in measure   **y** as in yes

- *Unvoiced (or aspirate) consonants* - the sound comes out on the breath and consequently the vocal cords are not drawn together.

e.g. **p** as in pen   **t** as in top   **f** as in few
   s as in sit   **k** as in kettle   **h** as in he
   ch as in chair   **th** as in mouth   **sh** as in she

Put your hand in front of your mouth - quite a bit of air explodes out onto your hand. This is important because this 'breathed' sound makes these consonant sounds carry.

Notice too how consonants are paired:
   p&b   t&d   f&v   s&z
   k&g   ch&j   th&th   sh&zh

Each pair is made in the same way, but one sound is made by the breath (unvoiced, aspirate), and the other one with sound (voiced or vocal). Experiment with these sounds - notice how they are formed. Hear and feel the difference between voiced/unvoiced consonants and develop your sensory awareness. These two categories are quite important as they add vibration or sharpness to the consonants. Become aware of the possibilities which you can use in your work.

Grade 2

Consonants also fall into another two categories - ***plosive*** or ***sustained***.

With the plosives, the passage of air or sound is stopped by either the lips or the tongue, and it is not until the muscles release the breath that we actually hear the sound. Plosive consonants cannot be *sustained* - the sound is not held on - they are made by the contact of two organs of speech, meeting and separating quickly:

e.g. p, b, t, d, k, g, ch, j.

With sustained consonants, the passage of air or sound is only partially stopped by the near contact of two organs of speech - the sound lasts until we run out of breath:

e.g. s, z, th, m, n, ng, l, r, f, v.

Notice how the voiced consonants take longer to say than the unvoiced and of course - sustained consonants take much longer to say than plosives. Have you realised that plosives can be both voiced/unvoiced and that sustained consonants can be both voiced/unvoiced? Enjoy discovering the physicality of sound - the difference between plosive and sustained sounds, appreciate the energy we use to give consonants impact and power. Then think about how and where we make the sounds.

Please note - you will *not* have to identify how these consonants are made. My own pupils have always enjoyed becoming aware of the muscularity of these sounds and how this knowledge has benefited their practical work - I hope you enjoy discovering their infinite possibilities too!

The Plosives - p & b, t & d, k & g, ch & j

- With p & b - the muscles press the lips together to stop the air coming out, they hold the sound for a moment, and when the lip muscles are released 'p' and 'b' explode out.

Grade 2

- With t & d - the tongue-tip is pressed against the ridge behind the teeth and held for a moment before being released.

- With k & g - it is the contact between the back of the tongue and the soft palate, and when the back of the tongue is released, the sound is released.

- With ch & j - it is the closing of the jaw and the tongue pressed against the teeth and hard palate that makes the stoppage.

The Sustained consonants - s & z, f & v, th & th, l, r, m, n, ng

- With s & z - the tip of the tongue is pressed against the teeth - the sound escapes down the channel in the centre of the tongue and through the spaces in the teeth.

- With f & v - the top teeth rest against the lower lip so that there is friction between the teeth and the lip as the breath escapes.

- With th & th - (as in the words thirty and those) - the tongue tip protrudes slightly through the teeth, friction is created between the teeth and the tongue tip as the sound comes out.

- l - made by placing the tip of the tongue against the gum ridge behind the top front teeth, stopping the sound there but with the sides of the tongue lowered, allowing the sound to escape and continue out through the mouth.

- r - made with the front of the tongue - curled up and slightly back, almost in contact with the hard palate - which gives the sound vibration.

- m - made by the lips pressed together, as 'p' & 'b'.

Grade 2

- n – made by the tongue tip pressing against the gum ridge behind the top front teeth.

- ng – made with the back of the tongue and soft palate, as 'k' & 'g'.

- With **m**, **n**, and **ng**, the soft palate comes down and the sound escapes through the nose. Put your hand just under your nose and feel the air coming down as you make the sound.

We are learning about the different categories of consonant sound so that you can *use* the sounds in your work - to colour words more effectively. Don't just learn the definitions and examples! For example in the words 'dread', 'grumble', 'moan' - when the consonant sounds are given their full value, we can achieve more imaginative effects.

Some words are more descriptive because of their sounds - in ***Onomatopoeia*** words use sounds to resemble or suggest the object or action. Think about 'slithering, sizzle, hiss, splash, buzz'. Images become clearer, more colourful ...we talk of 'word pictures'.

By becoming more aware of the dynamics of sounds in words we can use our voices to greater effect - think about wiggle, tiptoe, heave, creep, sneak, shiver, delicious. We need to reconnect to the sounds in words. In ***Alliteration***, words begin with the same consonant sound. Look how effective these advertising slogans were:

> *'Phyllosan fortifies the over forties.'*
> *'Findus frozen fish fingers are finest.'*
> *'Crawfords cream crackers taste so crisp and creamy.'*
> *'Rowntree's jelly - full of fresh fruit flavour.'*

The sound repetition makes an impression on our minds. Sound transfers into sight. Words create images. We aim for speech that is colourful, vital, full of positive energy - we realise its potential and become aware of an extra dimension to our work.

Below is a passage from *The Twits* by Roald Dahl - a chapter called 'The Wormy Spaghetti'. Enjoy the wonderful images which the words create in our imagination. By examining the components of our language, the picture transmitted is clearer, more colourful and, our ultimate aim, truer to the writer's intent. Everything you need to be more expressive is in the text - you just need to be more aware of the possibilities.

The Wormy Spaghetti

The next day, to pay Mr Twit back for the frog trick, Mrs Twit sneaked out into the garden and dug up some worms. She chose big long ones and put them in a tin and carried the tin back to the house under her apron.

At one o'clock, she cooked spaghetti for lunch and she mixed the worms in the spaghetti, but only on her husband's plate. The worms didn't show because everything was covered with tomato sauce and sprinkled with cheese.

'Hey, my spaghetti's moving!' cried Mr Twit, poking around in it with his fork.

'It's a new kind,' Mrs Twit said, taking a mouthful from her own plate which of course had no worms. 'It's called Squiggly Spaghetti. It's delicious. Eat it up while it's nice and hot.'

Mr Twit started eating, twisting the long tomato-covered strings around his fork and shovelling them into his mouth. Soon there was tomato sauce all over his hairy chin.'

It's not as good as the ordinary kind,' he said, talking with his mouth full. 'It's too squishy.'

'I find it very tasty,' Mrs Twit said. She was watching him from the other end of the table. It gave her great pleasure to watch him eating worms.

Grade 2

Finally, some exercises!

Muscles become lazy when not in use! We need to become more aware of the muscularity of the lips and tongue, the importance of relaxing and opening the jaw, unclenching teeth! Smile! Yawn! Pucker lips, stretch them back. Blow through the lips, vibrate the lips - make a sound resembling a horse when it shies: br-br-br!

- Chew an imaginary sticky toffee - use your tongue to pick it off your teeth!
- Lick your chin and cheeks with your tongue, like a cat, then move your tongue around the inside of your mouth.
- Tap your tongue against the hard palate - t, d, l, n - let those sounds really reverberate.
- Exaggerate the lip sounds - p, b, w, m, f, v - feel the vibrations.
- Exercise the soft palate at the back of the throat with k, g, ng - exaggerate these sounds, as they encourage the soft palate to move.

Now for some Tongue Twisters:

Before you begin - remember you need to *say them quickly and in a series of three*. They really do make you realise how agile our speech organs need to be!

Lips
p   Please prune plum trees promptly. (x 3)
b   A big bug bit a bold bald bear and the bold bald bear bled blood badly. (x 3)
w   War weary warriors. (x 6)
m   A missing mixture measure. (x 6)
f   Freckle-faced Freddie fidgets. (x 6)

Grade 2

Tongue Tip
- t   Thirty-three sly shy thrushes. (x 3)
- d   Does double bubble gum double bubble? (x 3)
- n   Nine nimble noblemen nibbled nuts. (x 3)
- l   literally literary. (x 6)
- th   Six thick thistles stuck together. (x 3)

Soft Palate and back of Tongue
- k   keenly cleaning copper kettles. (x 3)
- g   Greek grapes. (x 6)
- ng   The young singer was singing the wrong song. (x 3)

Grade 2

To summarise the main points

- We recognise a consonant sound because the sound is stopped or partially stopped by an organ of speech.

- A *voiced* consonant is made by the breath vibrating on the vocal cords which adds to the resonance of the sound.

- An *unvoiced* consonant is where the sound comes out on the breath - which makes the sound carry.

- With these two categories voiced / unvoiced we are made aware of the differences and how we can *use* these sounds in our work.

- Sustained consonants - here the sound is partially stopped and lasts until we run out of breath - words can be most effective when these sounds are given their full value e.g. sizzle, splash, hiss, buzz, shiver, sneak, delicious.

- Plosive consonants - the sound cannot be sustained, the passage of sound is completely stopped, it explodes out when the muscles are released. Plosives make us aware of the impact and power a word can have. e.g. plunge, propel, push, slump, leap, jump, boom, beat, break, bark, tear, took, hit, cut, bolt.

- We identify our speech organs, discover how and where speech sounds are made and can use this knowledge to create a more imaginative performance.

GRADE THREE

Candidates are asked about:
- **Phrasing.**
- **The neutral vowel and its value to speech, the terms 'monophthong' and 'diphthong'.**
- **Sense pauses.**
- **The candidate's own ideas about the differences between written and spoken English, that is "What can be expressed in spoken English that is missing in written English?"**

Let us first begin by defining a 'word'! A word consists of a sound or a combination of sounds - these sounds are vowels and consonants. We learn to speak by imitation - we know how to say a word because we hear it and we repeat the familiar pronunciation without much conscious thought. The problem only occurs when we come across a word that isn't familiar - so how do we pronounce it?

We are suddenly aware that words are divided into smaller units. Some of these units carry more weight than others - we call this the *main stress*, where we throw the main part of our voice in a word.

In order to communicate successfully, we have to feel confident that we can pronounce words we haven't come across before, we haven't heard before but only seen in print. We need to encourage candidates to increase their word power - to delve into the huge and expressive English Language.

Here is a sentence from *Alice's Adventures in Wonderland*, containing the word 'melancholy'. This word has caused many difficulties with pupils as it is no longer in common daily use and therefore, is rarely heard. Pupils tend to put the main weight of their voices on the second part of the word 'melancholy' instead of the first 'melancholy', which destroys the rhythm of the word and the sentence.

Grade 3

'.... and the poor little thing was waving its tail about in a melancholy way, being quite unable to move.'

As a general rule - nouns have their main (primary) stress on the *first* syllable of a word and verbs have their main stress on the *second* syllable of a word. Now I'll explain to you what a syllable is!

A syllable is a *word* or *part of a word*, which forms one sound, one unit of pronunciation, e.g. 'motion' contains 3 vowels, but only 2 vowel sounds and therefore 2 syllables.

For example:
    'book' contains 1 syllable (tap out the rhythms in each word)
    'reading' contains 2 syllables
    'discussion' contains 3 syllables
    'television' contains 4 syllables
    'communication' contains 5 syllables

A syllable contains a vowel sound. When we learn about syllables, we begin to understand how a word is pronounced - how a word has its own speech tune, its own rhythm - according to its main stress and secondary stresses. We start to think about choice of words, how writers are attuned to the sounds in words and choose words because of their particular rhythm as well as meaning. We are made aware of how writers use language to create speech patterns which are the *rhythms* of natural speech.

We can also alter the length of syllables and emphasise them to create *effects*. By studying the components of our language, we begin to appreciate its possibilities. This information will *not* be asked for by the examiner, but the information is valuable and should be absorbed!

Grade 3

This leads me on to explain **phrasing** and its purpose in our work. A phrase is a *group of words which form an idea*. A phrase reveals a writer's thought pattern - which we interpret orally. Each phrase *creates* an image reflected in our minds.

For example:
'I'd better take my umbrella / in case it rains.'
(Two phrases in one sentence).

We usually read and speak in phrases, not individual words - unless, of course, we want to create a deliberate effect, for instance, playing a character in distress with a disturbed frame of mind:

'If / you / don't / get / out of / my / house - I'll call / the police.'

Words and phrases should *flow*, there should be idea on idea, a *feeling of continuity* and a sense of a *build-up of interest*. We discover how a writer develops his ideas to a point of climax.

Sometimes a short sentence is said as a phrase:

'I've finished my homework.'

We are made aware of the natural rhythms of our speech. It is so *important* when reading a piece out aloud, especially during Sight Reading, *to look ahead* and *take in the phrase* to be spoken - not just the adjoining word.

Here is a long sentence from *The Lion, the Witch, and the Wardrobe* without any written punctuation, but containing several phrases:

'The sledge was a fine sight as it came sweeping towards Edmund with the bells jingling and the dwarf cracking his whip and the snow flying up on each side of it.'

Grade 3

In this sentence we have several phrases separated by ***sense pauses***. Written punctuation guides our eyes whilst we can explain 'sense pauses' as *oral punctuation, guiding our ears!* Often these sense pauses do correspond to written punctuation - but are not dependent on it. So we can define 'sense pauses' as the pauses used to separate phrases in a sentence. It is not necessary to pause for breath at these partial pauses - the tone of our voices is sustained as we pause. Notice how words are emphasised as we pause. We develop our 'listening' skills and become aware of the rhythms of our thought and speech patterns.

Here is the sentence again, showing the sense pauses (/):

> ***'The sledge was a fine sight / as it came sweeping towards Edmund / with the bells jingling / and the dwarf cracking his whip / and the snow flying up on each side of it.'***

Consider how effective this long sentence is with all the imagery and the excitement Edmund felt at suddenly seeing the sledge. Its effectiveness is due to the flow of the phrasing - how we can build up atmosphere and capture the flavour of the writing. Consider how it would sound if this sentence were to be read as several shorter sentences with more of a staccato effect - the result would be different and not as the writer intended.

Look at the words writers choose, how many words they use with one syllable, like a steady heartbeat, or words with several syllables. Look at the sentence construction - how many phrases, the length of the phrases, how long or short - all an insight into a writer's thought-pattern - for us to interpret. This in turn influences and develops our own creativity.

<u>*Grade 3*</u>

The terms 'monophthong' and 'diphthong'
In Grade One we defined and explained single and double vowels.

The term 'monophthong' comes from the Greek word meaning *'one sound'* the technical term for a single vowel sound. A complete, unaltered vowel sound. In Grade One we explained in some depth about short sounding and long sounding single vowels - *monophthongs*.

'Diphthong' means *'two sounds'* - the technical term for a double vowel sound - *two monophthongs blended together* and said in the same time it takes to make a long-sounding monophthong. The weight of our voices is always on the first part of the double vowel sound (diphthong). Look back to Grade One and see the explanation of how the various diphthongs are made up.

The neutral vowel and its value to speech
The neutral vowel is *a short-sounding single vowel* (monophthong) - think of the vowel sound in the word 'the' in this sentence, *'Th<u>e</u> table is laid'*.

The neutral vowel is both the *shortest* and *most commonly occurring vowel* sound in the English Language! It takes various forms of spelling - sof<u>a</u>, <u>a</u>bsurd, broth<u>er</u>, cupb<u>oa</u>rd - so listen to the sound in the words, don't be confused by the spelling.

It always occurs in an *unstressed* or *unaccented* syllable. By neutralising vowels in our words, our speech is not over-emphasised. An unnatural syllabic stress is avoided:

veget<u>a</u>ble	mount<u>ai</u>n	<u>a</u>fraid
c<u>o</u>ntinue	meth<u>o</u>d	estim<u>a</u>te

It *encourages* a natural flow to the rhythm of our speech.

<u>Grade 3</u>

We can also neutralise a word in a sentence to *change* the emphasis and therefore the *meaning* of the sentence, for example: "Do you want fish 'nd chips?" OR "Do you want fish <u>and</u> chips?"

There are some other examples of words of one syllable we can neutralize to alter the intention of our words: a, of, to, at, but, for, has, that, them, there, was, can, shall.

For instance - 'He <u>was</u> a good teacher' (emphasising good instead of was!)

The *more words* emphasised in a phrase or sentence, the *less effective* will be the emphasis, and so the neutral vowel is very important for the economy of language and the flow of natural colloquial speech.

Here is a piece from *The Secret Garden* - the neutral vowel is underlined. Listen to the effect the vowel makes and try not to let the spelling confuse you. I've also marked the sense pauses and phrases.

'Mary's heart b<u>e</u>gan t<u>o</u> thump / <u>a</u>nd her hands t<u>o</u> shake <u>a</u> little / in her d<u>e</u>light <u>a</u>nd excitem<u>e</u>nt./ Th<u>e</u> robin kept singing <u>a</u>nd twittering <u>a</u>way / <u>a</u>nd tilting his head t<u>o</u> one side, / <u>a</u>s if he were <u>a</u>s excit<u>e</u>d <u>a</u>s she w<u>a</u>s. / What w<u>a</u>s this und<u>e</u>r her hands / which w<u>a</u>s square <u>a</u>nd made <u>o</u>f iron / <u>a</u>nd which her fing<u>e</u>rs found <u>a</u> hole in.'

If the neutral vowel is not observed, we can sound over-precise, stilted, too formal and punctilious - unless of course we wish to re-create this characterisation in our pieces!

'I do not much dislike the matter, but the manner of his speech.'
Anthony and Cleopatra

Grade 3

Now to the differences between written and spoken English. Here are some of my own thoughts for you to consider.

All our examinations are concerned with the Spoken Word in one form or another. There are many advantages over the written word. Spoken English needs a more informal vocabulary - I am / I'm; I have / I've - we can sound friendlier!

We *neutralise* more vowels when speaking. We can *vary* the speed of delivery more easily. We can introduce effective pauses and vary different pause lengths. We can alter the pitch and volume within a piece. Using our voices we can stress syllables, varying the length and volume and pitch. We can emphasise key words and phrases more readily.

We can also use *facial expression and body language* to convey extra meaning. Though sometimes our choice of words can be ambiguous, the appropriate tone of voice and sympathetic body language usually *make the meaning clear* and help eliminate any possible misunderstanding, whereas when we rely only on the written word, we must make sure our meaning is exact. To illustrate this point there are over 100 entries listed in the Oxford Thesaurus under the heading 'good'. We need to be aware of the subtle shades of difference in meaning between each word.

And finally, remember it is much more difficult to ask someone to repeat something than it is to be able to read something again. We may read a story or poem over and over again but we rarely repeat the same spoken sentence!

To summarise the main points

- **Phrasing** - explains how we *group* words into thought-patterns. In our work we interpret these ideas orally. This develops fluency - we are made aware of the natural rhythms of speech.

- **Sense pauses** - written punctuation guides the eye when reading, sense pauses guide our ears to the natural pauses within a piece.

- **Neutral vowel** - most commonly occurring vowel sound and the shortest sound in the English Language. Our speech therefore is not over-emphasised, we avoid stressing unaccentuated syllables and this contributes to the natural rhythms of our speech.

GRADE FOUR

Candidates are asked about:
- **Breathing for Speech and Drama**
- **Inadequate methods of Breathing**

Our voice is the means by which we *communicate* our inner self. What do we aim to achieve?

a. to be heard (posture, relaxation, breathing);
b. to be understood (delivery via vocal skills);
c. to be clear (articulation - correct formation of vowels, consonants);

These topics will be explored in Grades Four, Five and Six.

For this Grade we need to concentrate on :
- to be **heard**; development of voice work as opposed to speech. Our voices are stimulated by an impulse from the brain, by an *intention* to speak and a *need* to communicate. Voice is produced by two elements - a flow of air and vibration. The air flow comes from breath.

Breath is the *energy* source of voice and speech. The way we breathe affects the rhythm and pace of our speech. Our aim is for our breath supply to be regulated in order to cope with phrasing and the sense of what we want to say. Our breathing dictates how much *energy* is available for the flow of words, *more energy* is needed for the *unvoiced* consonants than the *voiced* ones - they are made with greater muscular *effort*.

Consider how the frenetic pace of city life affects the speech tunes of urban dwellers compared with the slower and more musical speech tunes of those who live in the country. To speak well you need economical and well-controlled breathing. Relate your breathing pattern to what you have to say, your mood, what you want to get across. You will discover that we are able to use the elements of vocal expression more fully, owing to good breath control. Therefore the *rhythm of speech* is linked to breathing habits.

A brief outline of how the voice works

Breath is inhaled through the mouth and nose, passing down the windpipe into the lungs. The *rib cage*, containing the conical-shaped lungs, *expands* as breath enters and the dome-shaped *diaphragm*, which forms the base of the chest, *flattens downwards*, increasing the *capacity* for breath. The greatest expansion is in the area of the lower ribs - front and back - as the lungs are more spacious in their lower halves. The air leaving the lungs passes through various passages to the larynx (voice box) located at the top of the windpipe (trachea).

In the *larynx* (voice box) there are two pieces of elastic tissue stretching from the front to the back. These are called the *vocal cords*, a set of muscles which are half the size of a postage stamp. The vocal 'cords' are the folds of the lining membrane of the larynx near the opening of the glottis (which is the space at the upper end of the windpipe, between the vocal cords - affecting voice modulation through expansion or contraction).

As the breath is exhaled and returns up the trachea it encounters the closing vocal cords in the larynx. In overcoming their resistance the breath causes the edges of the folds to vibrate in the air stream to produce *voice*. (This is like the vibratory noise made when the neck of a balloon is held flat as air escapes). The vibrating columns of air are passed through the *main resonators* providing *tone quality* - these are the throat (pharynx), the mouth and the nose.

The vocal cords come together - or to use the technical term 'approximate' - *only when we are going to make sound*, when we breathe normally there is a space between them and the breath passes through freely. The sound waves of voice produced in the larynx are never heard as they are immediately modified by the spaces they pass through.

Grade 4

The *resonating* cavities of the pharynx, mouth and nose *amplify* the basic sound flow. The 'balance' in managing the resonant qualities of these spaces - directing the air flow appropriately for each sound - can make subtle variations in the *tone* of voice and *control* the carrying power (projection) of our voices. The dropping of the jaw and the shaping of the mouth have a strong effect in allowing voice to carry without strain. The hard palate *becomes a sounding board*. We realise that the *force* of the breath coupled with *well directed* sound is the *key* to *audibility*.

Relaxed, regular, deep breathing regulates the oxygen supply to the brain and aids clear thinking. Clarity of speech is often unconsciously connected to clarity of thinking. When the voice has comfortable, firm *breath support* it is flexible, reflects what we think, achieves improved *audibility*, and is full of positive energy - a greater *vitality* is reflected in the voice. We depend on the breath force to make the sound - too much makes the sound breathy, too little makes the attack glottal and the tone hard - therefore our breathing has to be well-controlled.

We need to *develop* a method of breathing for speech because we need a greater capacity of breath for inhalation, we need to increase the *control* over the muscles - so we have a steady outgoing supply of breath for sustaining the differing lengths of phrases and develop the *strength* of the muscles for the varying levels of volume and projection. We are using muscles that do not come into play during our day-to-day breathing.

Now we must explore how we *achieve* the most *effective* method of breathing for speech - *'the intercostal diaphragmatic method'* or *'centred breathing'*. I'll begin by explaining how good posture is vital for voice production.

A tense body is stiff, rigid. Shoulders are raised. Fists are clenched. Jaws are set. Tension stretches the vocal cords so that the sound is tight. Knees and legs tremble or are locked and rigid. Our breathing becomes erratic and our mouths dry up. Our speech is affected because our breathing is gasped and uncontrolled. The tone is hard - there is a lack of range and

Grade 4

vocal expression. Also, when we are tense and in a state of panic, we are not able to think clearly.

We need to aim for a relaxed body and mind - a positive attitude creates positive energy, and this spark is a vital element in communicating. I cannot over-emphasise the importance of mind/body unity. Remember too that the first impression we give is a visual one.

> *'I think, therefore I am.'*
> **Descartes**

To explore and develop the natural potential of our voices - we must first free our body from unnecessary tension. Poor posture, besides reflecting a poor bodily image, will restrict the power of our voices. Chins thrust forward, craning necks, tightly clenched jaws restrict the space in which our voices can resonate (resound). It is important to keep the airways free. Slumping or raised shoulders, or curved backs, restrict our rib cages and we lose control over our breathing. We should aim for a natural alignment of our bodies, checking our head-neck-spine position (the *Alexander Technique* is based on this principle).

This technique is so relevant to our work because it is concerned with mis-use of the body and how this is reflected in our voices. Incidentally, most Drama school courses explore the Alexander Technique and many of the major theatre companies use this method of body alignment during the rehearsal period. If our backs are not straight the ribs cannot open properly, and there is little possibility of movement at the bottom of the rib cage. Many yoga techniques also provide wonderful insights into these issues.

Grade 4

The Alexander Technique explored

Frederick Mattias Alexander (1869-1955) was an actor, and through a complaint which threatened his career he developed a technique to help take the strain out of our hectic, stressful lives. His voice failed him repeatedly during performance. He began to notice (actors need to be compulsively introspective) that he tightened his neck as he spoke and his head tilted backwards.

Alexander's theory is that *mind and body* are essentially one. The way we *use* our bodies can affect how we ultimately feel about ourselves. For example, we hunch our shoulders when angry, wring our hands when nervous or tense. Fear, anxiety, tension and stress - typical examination symptoms! - can make us adopt wrong postures. These mannerisms influence how our minds *and* bodies function. The way we *use* our bodies can affect how we ultimately feel about ourselves. Laughter is important for a feeling of well-being and expansion of the ribs.

The Alexander Technique is basically a series of physical movements designed to correct bad posture and bring the body back into alignment. It consists of *unlearning* bad habits acquired over many years. The technique can alleviate mental, emotional and physical conditions, through correction of the *physical* imbalance. We also have to acquire the habit of positive thinking and realise we cannot separate mind and body.

We need to be made aware that we can lengthen and widen the spine and torso: the neck should be free from tension - lengthen it out by nodding the head gently up and down. If the shoulders are dropped forward, the head compensates by being pulled back, therefore the resonating space in the neck is squashed. The most common mis-use is pulling the head back and down, tightening the neck, shortening the back - which leads to mis-use elsewhere!

Grade 4

Here are some typical Alexander Technique exercises for you to incorporate in your work.

1. Breathe out on a whispered 'ah' to widen the back and open up the throat and jaw.

2. To become aware of the relationship of the head and neck to the rest of the body - imagine a cord is coming out of the top of your head, pulling you upward. SMILE! This lengthens and widens the back.

3. Sit on a chair, take in breath, bend until your stomach drops down and touches your thighs - this opens up the back! I find that this activity is always accompanied by much laughter - which is in itself an excellent relaxation exercise!

We depend on the resonating cavities for the *quality* of sound - this is the *amplification* of our primary note - the vibrations in the larynx are magnified in the hollows of the throat and mouth - two equally important elements are needed - we must have *space* and a *sounding board* for projecting the voice - good posture is therefore VITAL!

Exercises designed for *relaxation* are based on sudden changes from tension to vigorous activity to an inert, relaxed state. We aim for a *balanced body* as every part of us is relevant to voice. We need to rid the body of any unnecessary tension, as tension is wasted energy; energy we need for communicating.

1. Head evenly balanced on spine (The head weighs approximately 14lbs - think about balancing a boulder on the neck of a vase!).
   Jaw free (yawn).
   Shoulders - if raised will tighten throat.
   Spine - don't slump or be too rigid.
   Stomach - don't hold in.
   Knees - unlock.
   Feet - firmly placed on the floor, slightly apart.

Grade 4

2. We'll repeat this - lying down, which encourages the back to be opened out.
   Lie on the floor, with knees bent, head resting on 2 or 3 books.
   Back spread.
   Shoulders spread and free.
   Lengthen down to the bottom of the spine.
   Elbows free.
   Wrists free.
   Neck free and lengthen out the back, jaw free.
   Tense and relax each muscle alternately to become aware of muscular tension and freedom.

The Alexander Technique seeks to establish a resting position in which all the joint surfaces are lengthening away from each other. To check posture, line up against a wall, head, shoulder blades, buttocks and heels touching the wall - walk away! You'll find that this is a very difficult posture to maintain!

Here are some relaxation exercises:

1. Lie on your back, feet together, arms by your side, hands lightly curled, fingers pointing towards the body. Close your eyes. Imagine a spark of life is travelling through each part of your body - starting at the toes - we tense as it enters our limbs and relax when it moves on. Imagine the spark is our energy source - alternatively feeling recharged and drained.

   Remain on the floor. Imagine *feeling* and seeing colours - red, orange, yellow then green, blue and ice white - let your mind react to the warmth through to the bitter cold and back to the warmth again.

2. *The Wave exercise* - which needs a partner or ideally works best with a group. This opens up the rib cage, promotes deep breathing, establishes eye contact and most importantly encourages laughter - which is good exercise for the diaphragm. Imagine you are trying to catch the attention of another person - you think you've met them before and

Grade 4

want to say Hello! Start off waving and saying "Hello" rather timidly, with intermittent eye contact - through to a confident, smiling "Hello" with established eye contact.

Tension through nervousness can be alleviated through preparation, practice and concentration which gives us a sense of being in *control*. A more positive attitude can be adopted if we remember that we are always performing to individuals - even if our audience is made up of rather a lot of individuals!

Our voices work best when all the resonating spaces in our body (chest, throat, mouth, nose) are fully open and the vibrating surfaces are free. We rely on the resonating spaces for the quality of sound we produce and this depends on our *posture* and *relaxation*.

The *power* of our voices is the breath. We need a *sufficient* amount of air taken in and then exhaled in an easy *controlled* manner. With lower chest breathing, the lungs are more spacious in their lower halves. The rib cage is also more flexible and less enclosed. The upper section is more rigid being attached to the breast bone (sternum). The chest (thorax) contains the lungs and heart. The thorax is a bony, cage-like structure consisting of the spinal column running down the back, the sternum or breast bone running down the front, the ribs, the shoulder blades and the collar bones.

The thorax contains 12 pairs of ribs. The top 5 pairs of ribs are attached firmly back and front, at the back of the spine and in the front to the breastbone. So if we take breath into the upper part of the chest, the whole rib cage has to move - there is not much room for air. Breathing in the upper chest also makes for a lot of tension in the neck and shoulders.

You will see there is considerable room for movement in the bottom half of the chest - partly because the chest is wider there and partly because the ribs are attached only to the spine at the back and connected by cartilage to the back bone. The bottom two pairs of ribs are unattached in front, they are

Grade 4

smaller than the other ribs and are called 'floating ribs'. The arrangement of the *ribs* is such that, when you breathe in, the muscles between the ribs (the *intercostals*) contract, enabling the bottom 7 pairs of ribs to swing upwards and outwards.

The opening of the back during breathing in is important, if we wish to use the lungs to their fullest capacity. Therefore this is the area on which we concentrate the breathing exercises. The action of the *diaphragm* also enlarges the chest and makes room for more air. The diaphragm is a large dome-shaped sheet of muscle placed so that it is like the floor of the chest, separating the cavities of the thorax and abdomen and in terms of surface area is the largest muscle in the body. The diaphragm is attached to the two floating ribs at its edges so that, as they swing out, the diaphragm is drawn out and flattened, enlarging the chest downwards. By exercise we can make the diaphragm descend lower and so draw air more deeply into the lungs.

Our lungs are protected by the thorax. We have two lungs, semi-circular in shape, each divided into lobes. The lungs consist of spongy tissue made up of air tubes and sacs, intermingling with these air sacs are millions of tiny blood vessels. It is here that the exchange of carbon dioxide for oxygen takes place and oxygen enters the blood to be circulated around the body.

These sacs and lungs are *inert* bodies - they do not have the power to perform any muscular activity and are not capable of taking in any air by themselves. The lungs store the air, the air must be *forced* into the lungs. If the thorax is increased in size, then the outside air pressure forces air into the lungs - the lungs follow the shape of the rib cage.

Grade 4

How is the thorax enlarged?

The whole breathing cycle is called respiration.

- During *inhalation* (breathing in)
  Muscles move bones. The intercostal muscles move the ribs. These muscles lie between the adjacent ribs and by contraction they lift the ribs upwards and outwards. We have *two sets* of intercostal muscles, one set to pull the ribs out and a second set to pull them in again. For *breathing in*, the *outer* intercostals contract, expanding the rib cage. **Remember** - *outer* intercostals move the rib cage *outwards*.

  The *diaphragm* is very important for *inhalation*. It forms the floor of the thorax and the roof of the abdomen. At the centre of the diaphragm is the central tendon which is pulled down during inhalation increasing the dimensions of the thorax, providing extra space for the lungs to be filled with air. The lungs are concave and follow the shape of the inside of the chest cavity.

- When *exhaling* (breathing out)
  With the more conscious and controlled breathing for speech - the *second set of intercostals* is brought into play. These are the *inner* intercostals. When they contract, pulling the ribs downwards and *inwards* - (there is also a sideways expansion as well as front and back) - air is *forced* out of the lungs. **Remember** - *the inner intercostals pull the ribs inwards*.

  To exhale, the diaphragm must rise again. Another set of muscles - *the abdominal muscles* - is required - these are important for *exhalation*. These muscles form the wall of the abdomen. The transverse abdominal muscles, run around the body like a *girdle*. When we breathe out, the abdominal muscles contract and pull in the abdominal wall. The contents of the abdomen are squeezed slightly and push up on the lower side of the diaphragm. With increasing

Grade 4

contraction of the abdominal muscles, the diaphragm rises under control. This is also known as the *abdominal press*.

The breathing is in two cycles - the movement of the thorax and the diaphragmatic action. We learn that there are 3 important sets of muscles for the intercostal diaphragmatic method of breathing for speech - the intercostals, the diaphragm and the abdominal muscles.

When extra control is needed during performing, or *extra* breath force is needed for projection, a slight modification to the intercostal method is made, especially useful for Music Theatre candidates. This method is called *rib-reserve breathing*.

This method relies on the separation of these two movements - the rib movement and the diaphragmatic movement. The thorax is expanded and the diaphragm lowered for breathing in. The abdominal muscles contract, indirectly controlling the rise of the diaphragm. Instead of the ribs returning to their original position they are held out by the prolonged contraction of the *outer* intercostals. The lungs consequently retain a *reserve of air*.

A replenishment of air then takes place as the diaphragm lowers, to be followed by a further contraction of the abdominal muscles during exhalation. There is a pumping action by the diaphragm as the thorax is kept expanded.

I should point out that the subject of rib-reserve breathing is quite controversial amongst many voice teachers today. They feel that extra tension is encouraged by the prolonged extension of the ribs. Yet, many singing and opera students advocate this method. Experiment and use this method to suit *your* needs.

There are many *advantages* to both methods:
1. the lungs are quickly replenished with sufficient air,
2. there is good control over the diaphragm by the abdominal muscles - so that there is an even flow of air,

3. the methods avoid gasping for air at the end of long phrases,
4. good firm breath support aids projection,
5. sufficient air supply and good control of the outgoing breath ensures that the dropping of the voice at the end of phrases is eliminated,
6. no strain is placed on the larynx.

Inadequate methods for Speech and Drama

1. ***Tidal breathing*** is used when we are resting or asleep but not actually speaking. It is rhythmical but doesn't call into play the controlled *conscious* movements of the muscles for the intercostal diaphragmatic method. The diaphragm sinks very slightly and the lower ribs move outwards a little by the action of the outer intercostals. Air is forced out by the *falling weight* of the ribs and the *recoil action* of the lungs.

2. ***Abdominal breathing*** occurs when the *diaphragm* sinks too low (approx. 3½" compared with 1½" for the intercostal diaphragmatic method). Consequently the abdominal contents are pushed down and the abdominal wall *protrudes*. The ribs are not used very much for expansion of the thorax - the intercostals therefore are not brought into play here. On breathing out, the *abdominal muscles* haven't enough control over the rising diaphragm - which *spring* back - letting the breath out in a gust. The sound escapes in a breathy rush and therefore does not vibrate the vocal cords properly.

3. ***Clavicular breathing*** (associated with the collar bones) or upper chest breathing is not recommended. Shoulders are drawn upwards as well as the breast bone and ribs. The diaphragm is squeezed out of action because the *thorax* becomes *narrow*. Only the upper part of the thorax is used - so there is little air intake into the lungs. The breathing is shallow and uncontrolled, the tone is strained and the speaker appears out of breath. Clavicular breathing also results in facial strain and general tension.

Grade 4

Breathing Faults

1. If insufficient air is taken in - gasping at the ends of phrases when speaking out on the breath flow may result - followed by noisy inhalation.
2. Dropping of the voice at the end of sentences - avoided by maintaining the pressure of the abdominal muscles when exhaling.
3. A tremolo may be heard. There is a wobble in the tone of the voice and is caused by a lack of smooth contraction of the abdominal muscles.
4. A rebound occurs when the breath flow continues after the final sound in the phrase, e.g. bad-uh.
5. A slow control by the abdominal muscles is needed to avoid breathy tone, when too much breath is expelled with aspirate consonants (p, t, f, k, s). Make sure that you haven't adopted a pattern of taking a deep breath in, *holding* the breath, and then when the breath is exhaled, the sound comes out in a breathy, uncontrolled stream.

Breathing Exercises (for capacity of the lungs and control of the abdominal muscles and diaphragm).

We have to start making a *conscious* effort in breathing for speech purposes to develop the muscles that govern it. When practising these exercises remember to go through the relaxation exercises first - check head-neck-spine alignment, relax the jaw - ensure that the shoulders are not raised when taking in breath and keep the lower abdominal muscles braced but without a feeling of tension.

Exercises help control stress and develop voice control. The rhythm of speech is linked to breathing habits - when nervous, our breathing patterns change - our breathing becomes shallow. When deep breathing though, be careful not to breathe too quickly, otherwise you will hyperventilate and become giddy.

Grade 4

An exercise to practise whilst walking! Think about breathing from your centre, breath *in*, stomach *out*; breath *out*, stomach *in*. Focus breathing on the *out* breath, sigh out or yawn.

1. **Exercise to establish the movement of the ribs and diaphragm.**

   When breathing in, imagine you are *drawing* or taking the breath in - this helps to keep the shoulders relaxed. Standing up, breathe in and raise the arms outwards and upwards until they are stretched above the head. The movement of the arms will assist the movement of the ribs and help to sustain them in a raised position during the next part of the exercise. While the arms are raised *pant* in and out three times. The stomach will move in and out. The arms should then be lowered slowly as further breath is exhaled. For further control, slow the intake and expiration of the breath - while the arms are raised.

2. **Exercise for Capacity and Control**

   We need to increase the amount of breath taken and develop the control to sustain longer phrasing in speech.

   Using the ribs only. Breathe in for a slow count of three. Pause and then breathe out gently with an open mouth - for a count of six. Raise the arms out to the sides, reaching shoulder height - on breathing in and lower them slowly while breathing out.

   Repeat but whisper the numbers on breathing out.

   Extend the counting to 9, 12, 15.

   Place the palms of the hands on the lower ribs and breathe in easily. Feel the ribs swing out. Gently blow the air out on an 'oo' sound and feel the ribs swing in. Repeat, sustaining the 'oo' sound for a count of 10.

<u>Grade 4</u>

Breathe in, raising the ribs (if this phrase makes you raise your shoulders as well - then think about drawing in breath, using the ribs). Whisper the following:

1 & 1	are 2	breathe
2 & 2	are 4	
4 & 4	are 8	breathe in again
8 & 8	are 16	
16 & 16	are 32	breathe in again
32 & 32	are 64	
64 & 64	are 128	

Repeat with voice.

Repeat and exhale on a sustained *mmmmm* (feel the vibration on your lips)

Repeat and exhale on a sustained *sssssssss*

Using the ribs and diaphragm, breathe in on the ribs and keep them expanded. Breathe in on the diaphragm and say 'January'. Follow this with further breaths on the diaphragm before saying each of the months of the year. The reserve of air in the ribs should be retained until you have spoken 'December'. Aim to speak all the months of the year using the air retained by the ribs.

3. Exercise for Power

To develop the strength of the muscles to develop volume of voice.

Don't push up the pitch of your voice when you want to increase volume. Projection depends on: force of breath, clarity of consonants, muscular energy with which we form our words.

Grade 4

Breathe in on the ribs, breathe in on the diaphragm. Using the air from the diaphragm count up to ten slowly, gradually increase the volume.

Breathe in on the ribs and diaphragm.

Let the breath go from the diaphragm on a loud, open sigh on an 'oo' sound. Follow this with an 'ee' sound using the air from the ribs.

For younger candidates:

1. Take a straw and a glass of water. Inhale and blow through the straw into the water. Make the flow of bubbles as regular as possible. Repeat controlling the bubbles slowly then increase the rate. This is a good exercise for breath flow.

2. Controlled breath force. Hold a sheet of paper about 8" from your mouth. Hold it by the top corners so that the paper hangs down freely. Blow gently towards the bottom of the sheet to make it swing away from you. Repeat blowing fiercely - when more force is needed - imagine the breath is coming from your stomach - the centre, and use your stomach as a trampoline.

   Repeat, holding the sheet at different distances from your mouth.

All the exercises mentioned are excellent - provided we can make the time to do them! However, these are only suggestions for you to consider - what is important is the underlying principle behind all these exercises.

We have to be realistic in our expectations - I am convinced that daily brisk walking is an ideal exercise for speech purposes too! When faced with a stressful situation, take a few, slow, controlled breaths *OUT!* Sighing or yawning as you breathe out

Grade 4

relaxes the throat too! Exercise releases endorphins in the brain, giving us a feeling of well-being and confidence.

Remember we spoke about the mind/body unity - how we feel about ourselves is reflected in our posture, which in turn affects our breathing, which affects the volume and pitch and the tone of our voice and the ability to think clearly - to be able to communicate effectively.

To summarise the main points

- We need to develop a method of breathing for speech purposes because we must strengthen muscles which do not come into play in our normal day-to-day breathing. Therefore we need to develop a method which provides the voice with *power* (projection) and *duration* (regulating the breath supply to *cope* with what you need to say).

- *Breath* is the *initial* impulse to make voice, and it is the *force* of this breath coupled with our ability to *direct the sound* efficiently into the cavities of the main resonators: throat and mouth...that is the *key* to *audibility*. Please make sure you *practise* the breathing exercises - they will make a huge difference to the quality of your work.

- Good posture is *vital* for effective voice production. Poor posture, besides reflecting a poor bodily image - will restrict the power of our voices. The first impression we give is a *visual* one. A positive attitude creates positive energy which is reflected in our voices. Concentrate on the mind/body unity. Please *work* on the relaxation exercises, don't just learn them!

- Aim for a natural alignment of your body - check the head-neck-spine position. Shoulders relaxed, jaws free.

- We depend on the *resonating* cavities for the *quality of sound* - and two equally important elements are needed - we must have *space* and a *sounding* board for the *amplification* of our voice - therefore once again REMEMBER good posture is VITAL!

- Lower chest breathing - technically known as the '*intercostal diaphragmatic*' method of breathing - ensures that we have greater *capacity* of breath for *inhalation* - the rib cage moves upwards and *outwards* by the *outer* intercostal muscles. At the same time the diaphragm descends - creating more *space* for the lungs to expand with air. With the *outgoing* breath needed for speech, we develop and strengthen the muscles for sustaining differing lengths of phrases and for volume and projection. When *breathing out* the abdominal muscles contract and the diaphragm rises under control. The *inner* intercostals pull *in* the rib-cage so that it resumes its usual position.

- The *diaphragm* consisting of a large dome-shaped sheet of muscle (and is considered the largest muscle in the body in terms of surface area) is very important for *inhalation*.

- The *intercostals*, muscles which lie between the ribs, move the *rib-cage* upwards and outwards.

- The *abdominal* muscles are very important for *exhalation* - they ensure a steady controlled outgoing supply of breath.

- Become aware that *inhalation* is normally the same process each time but *exhalation* can be *different*, depending on the *use* to which you put your breath.

- *Inadequate methods* - Tidal, Abdominal and Clavicular - do not call into play the controlled *conscious* movements of the muscles employed by the intercostal diaphragmatic method.

- Effective breathing ensures that we have an adequate oxygen supply to our brains to aid clear thinking; it has an effect on the tone, range and pitch of our voices which in turn contribute towards successful communication.

Grade 4

GRADE 4 WRITTEN PAPER

1. Definition and recognition of vowel sounds - covered in Grade One.
2. Monophthongs and diphthongs - covered in Grade Three.
3. Definition of consonant sounds and their classification under voiced or unvoiced, vocal or aspirate - covered in Grade Two.
4. Inter-costal diaphragmatic breathing: the parts of the body involved, the process and the application - covered in Grade Four.
5. Definition of a phrase - covered in Grade Three.
6. Accentuation and inflection (see below).
7. The candidate's own views on the difference between written and spoken English: some ideas to consider - covered in Grade Three.

Accentuation and Inflection

In *accentuation* we have the *main stress* (weight of our voice) on a syllable of a word *to aid pronunciation*.

We emphasise part of the word to make clear its meaning

e.g. re<u>cord</u>, <u>rec</u>ord   <u>in</u>sult, ins<u>ult</u>   present,pre<u>sent</u>
      <u>con</u>duct, con<u>duct</u>   <u>sur</u>vey, sur<u>vey</u>   <u>con</u>test, cont<u>est</u>

A frequently mis-pronounced word with my own students is 'the<u>saur</u>us' - listen to what happens to the rhythm of the word when the wrong syllable is accented - <u>the</u>saurus. A general guideline is that nouns have their main (primary) stress on the first syllable and verbs have their primary stress on the second syllable.

We also notice that some words are spelt the same but they sound different because the weight of our voices is attached to the accented syllable, which changes according to the word's meaning. When speaking we usually change the *pitch* on the accented syllable, usually upwards. The accented syllable can be emphasised using volume or we can hold the duration of the

Grade 4

syllable for a longer time. In words of more than one syllable we have a primary stress and a secondary stress, making us aware of speech patterns and the natural rhythms of speech, e.g. "we are going to pre*sent* the headmistress with her leaving *present*".

Inflections are the *glides in pitch*, upwards or downwards, on single words. We are mainly concerned with the inflections on words that *end* phrases and sentences. A statement ends with a falling inflection and is used for questions which begin with a question word. The voice glides down from the original pitch of the last syllable of the word in the phrase or sentence - involving a gradual weakening of tone.

A rising inflection is used to connect ideas and at the end of questions which do not have a question-word:

    Has he go↗ne ?

    Appl↗es, orang↗es, p↗ears, and..........................

The voice glides up in pitch from the preceding syllable spoken.
A *rising* inflection generally indicates that the thought is *incomplete* and *implies doubt* and *uncertainty*. A *falling* inflection indicates that the thought is *complete* and implies *certainty* and *finality*.

Inflection expresses *meaning*, it is not used for variety or effect. We *listen* to the *implications suggested* by the *sounds* in our voices, the words therefore become secondary.

See Grade Five notes for a fuller explanation.

GRADE FIVE

Candidates are asked about:
- **Speech colour, to include pitch, pace, pause, inflection, tone and power.**
- **Examples to illustrate answers.**

The elements of Vocal Variety - pitch, pace, pause, inflection, tone and power - are the six main facets of *vocal expression*. We use them to add *colour* to our speech so we may be *understood*, and to *enhance* the text we are interpreting. As we move through each one of them in turn, you will see that many of them are linked. A general rule must be that the subject matter always dictates the choice.

Use of the Speaking voice

The aim is to:
- be *heard* (posture, relaxation, breathing) - covered in Grade Four.
- to be *clear* (articulation, crispness of consonants, word endings) explained in Grade Two and explored further in Grade Six.
- to be *understood* (delivery via vocal skills) - to be explored in the following pages.

For a successful performance/presentation we have to take into consideration:
- the **words** we use
- our voices - to enhance the words we use
- our body language - to reinforce the words we use

When *developing* any new skill, we must undergo the following sequence: awareness, understanding, practice, and experience.

Grade 5

I shall now explain each element of Vocal Variety and how we can *apply* them to our work.

PITCH

This is the height and depth of our voices. We can say there are three main *general* pitch levels - 'middle' for our usual conversational tone. 'High' for excitement, happiness, hysteria. 'Low' for sadness, controlled rage, thoughtfulness. Men have naturally lower pitched voices than women. There are several technical uses of change of pitch level: accentuation, emphasis, a change of thought or an emotional involvement.

1. ***Accentuation***

    The change of pitch on a *syllable* in a word. Most multi-syllabic words receive prominence on one or more of their syllables. We change the pitch on the accentuated syllable, usually *upwards*.

    e.g. succeéd, télephone, atténtion.

    Accentuation can *also* alter the meaning of words spelt the same - therefore it is an aid to pronunciation,

    e.g. récord, recórd; présent, presént; éxtract, extráct; résearch, reséarch.

    We can also create atmosphere by *lowering* the pitch on the accentuated syllable, to obtain the effect we want to achieve,

    e.g. detest, disgusting, grumpy.

<u>Grade 5</u>

2. *Emphasis*

Whereas '*accentuation*' is stress upon a *syllable* in a word, '*emphasis*' is the stress given to a *whole word* in a phrase or sentence.

We can underline the important word in a phrase by a change of pitch on that word, e.g. 'This is the best of the three-roomed flats' x 4 interpretations.

When we use 'antithesis' (words emphasised by *opposite* ideas) the pitch changes from high to low:

"I want the r̷ed shoes, not the blu̷e!"

The pitch change on the word emphasised is either higher or lower than the rest of the sentence.

Use the subject matter to decide, but remember that an *overstressed* phrase or sentence loses its impact! This alternation of stress and pitch change contributes to the natural rhythm of delivery.

3. *Change of Thought*

We introduce a *change of pitch* to reflect a *change of thought* - say at the beginning of a new paragraph, a new idea or the beginning of a message. A *higher pitch* introduces a bright, lively tone and a lower pitch introduces a more serious topic. We lift our voices when listing points - 1st, 2nd, 3rd. A change to a *lower pitch* is required to introduce a *parenthesis* (a word or phrase inserted into a sentence as an after thought - the sentence is grammatically correct without it, usually marked by commas),

e.g. Judi Dench,   collapsed on stage.
        the leading actress,

Grade 5

4. *Emotional Involvement*

The artistic use of pitch: 'high' pitch for excitement, anticipation, hysterical anger; 'low' pitch for low spirits, dejection, sorrow, tiredness as well as mystery, fear and contained anger. We must aim for *variety* - a 'high pitch' adopted for too long eventually loses its impact, as our ears close off to the high frequency.

Consider pitch and *characterisation*, male and female, young and old. When playing two characters, change the pitch to indicate change of speakers, also a change from narrative to dialogue. Use the *subject matter* to guide you and your *ear* to decide what is *effective*.

PACE

This is the *variation* of the rates used in delivery and one of the most difficult skills to achieve: many candidates adopt a pace in their pieces and maintain this pace *throughout*. A regular pace is quite soporific! It is dependent upon the speaker's ability to articulate well, the speaker's ability to make the *meaning* clear, the subject matter, our audience, our venue.

We aim for *variety* of pace to *maintain interest*:
- faster/slower (need contrast)
- sense of urgency, exciting, go faster/higher
- dramatic - slow and low
- parenthesis - go slower
- slower - serious subject, end of message, the end of your pieces, so that the audience knows you are finishing.

1. We can alter the *duration of syllables* within a word, achieved by *dwelling* on long vowel sounds and sustained consonants, e.g. alone, weary, sweeping.

Grade 5

2. To *emphasise* a whole word or phrase - choose a *different rate* from the *main pace* of the phrase or sentence. We are looking for *contrast* - usually a slower rate is used, e.g. The chances of winning the lottery are remote! x 4 interpretations.

   - *Speed up* on *unimportant* words and phrases, including a parenthesis.
   - *Slow down* on place names, people's names, products - to *highlight* these.

Pitch and *pace* are linked. We usually quicken our voices with a higher pitch and slow down with a lower pitch. If your extract or poem reaches a climax, the pace should quicken, along with a change of pitch, to *emphasise* the climax.

Artistically, the choice of rate, as pitch, is bound up with *emotion*. An excited state of mind is reflected in a quicker rate of delivery, a more serious mood commands a slower delivery - we are guided by *our imaginations*!

POWER
The power of the voice is not *dependent* on the *loudness* of the voice, in fact the effect is more often achieved by using a quieter tone but with greater articulation, we need sharper diction. Too much volume eventually loses its impact - our ears close off to the sound! Its effect depends upon the emotions and the dramatic intensity of the spoken word.

As with pitch and pace, *power* can be used for the *accentuation* of syllables, to *emphasise* a word. Gradual increase of power, together with an increase of pitch and pace on successive phrases can help to create vocal climax and create the rhythmical patterns of our speech.

Grade 5

Here are some examples to increase your awareness of the value of power, coupled with a variety of pitch and pace.

> *'I'm too excited to speak!'*
> *'Listen, and keep very still, there's someone creeping about outside'.*

PAUSE

Pause suggests change of thought, a change of situation, it helps create atmosphere. Good use of pause - *silence* - can be as *effective* as *good use of words*. We have discussed its importance for breathing. Pauses may be long or short - we must re-create in performance an interval of time for a character's thought or reflection, which would be natural in spontaneous speech. This underlines the importance of *ear training* - the ability to listen and appreciate the *value of pause*.

a. **Sense pauses**
   (covered in Grade Three in depth)

   When phrases are spoken with pauses in between, the rhythm in speech is achieved. Breath is not necessarily taken at these partial pauses as the tone *can be held* through a pause. We can speak many phrases on one breath - though we would breathe at the end! Punctuation marks refer to print and not to speech - so we do not say that phrases are separated by commas but by sense pauses.

b. *Dramatic pauses* **for effect**
   (Drama/prose)

- The *rhetorical* pause - a pause placed *before* a word to make your audience wonder or *anticipate* what is going to follow. (The r in 'rhetorical' and the b in 'before' are both *consonants* - which will help you remember this definition!).

   Example: I want that boy to / leave the classroom.

Grade 5

- The *oratorical* pause - a pause placed *after* a word to make your audience reflect on what has been said. (The o in 'oratorical' and the a in 'after' are both vowels - to help you remember!)

    Example: There is a tide / in the affairs of men.

- The *emotional* pause - used to indicate a disturbed state of mind due to extreme sorrow or anger. This pause is placed anywhere in the sentence to emphasise the illogical state of mind.

    Example: I am / so / angry I can / hardly / speak.

c. **Some more effective uses for pause**

1. Before and *after* 'direct speech' - wait before continuing with the narrative.
2. Grammatical commas, full stops, before a paragraph, aim to vary the length of pauses.
3. Before and after: names, figures or statistics; to *highlight* these points, used with pace and pitch.
4. Quotes, reported speech.

Verse pauses will be explained in Grade Seven.

INFLECTION

When explaining *pitch* we said a *change of pitch* up or down is used to *emphasise* a syllable in accentuation or a *whole word* for emphasis.

Examples: t<u>e</u>lephone ↗
are you going <u>out</u> now?

We can define pitch as a *leap* in the *notes of the voice* to produce emphasis and variety in delivery.

Inflection is the gentle rise and fall of the voice on the syllables of the words *within* the *pitch*. Therefore one may use falling

Grade 5

inflections within a high pitch and rising inflections within a low pitch without any change of pitch level. The pattern should reflect thoughts and feelings, emotions. So we define *inflection* as the sliding of the voice from one note to another on a single word. We are mainly concerned with the inflections on words that *end* sentences and phrases.

Inflection suggests the *implication in our voice* - it expresses *meaning*, it is not used for variety or effect.

Simple Inflections
Glide upwards or downwards on single words. These inflections are often heard when answering the telephone:

Example:

(Hello) "yes" (Is that you Rebecca?) "yes" reply is confirmed.

A *rising inflection* generally indicates that the thought is incomplete and so connects one idea to the next. It is used in questions which do not *begin* with question-words. It also implies doubt and uncertainty. The voice *glides up* in pitch from the preceding syllable spoken.

Examples:
We bought apples, peaches, bananas (the list is incomplete - we are waiting to *hear* another item)

Are you going? (question without a question-word)

Perhaps (doubt)

A *falling inflection* indicates that the thought is *complete*, therefore it serves to disconnect ideas. A statement ends with a falling inflection. It is used in questions which begin with question-words (where, which, what, when, why). It also implies certainty and finality. The voice *slides down* from the original pitch of the last syllable of the word.

Grade 5

Examples:
  We bought the app<u>les</u> (complete)

  Where are you go<u>ing</u>? (question with a question-word)

  Y<u>es</u>! (certainty)

We *usually* use two glides in the voice - either down-up or up-down (the inflection is named according to its final turn). These are named **Double Inflections**. If *double inflections* are used there is an *extra meaning implied*.

Examples:
- Will you be at the meeting tonight ?

- Reply - yes (doubtful yes)

- Reply - yes (of course, do you need to question me at all!)

Compound Inflections
Used for irony, sarcasm, incredulity, satire - used with even more extreme emotions and *deeper implications than the words can convey*. Three slides of the voice are used.

Examples:
- Have you heard about Max?

- Reply: 'yes' (and I know more about it than you do!)

- Reply: 'yes' (I should like you to tell me, I'm not too sure I know the full details)

Grade 5

To summarise

Simple inflections are for simple ideas, double or compound inflections whenever the *sense* is *deeper than the actual words conveyed*. We can have simple rising/falling, double rising/falling, and compound rising/falling inflections.

Some examples for you to practise:

Statements

- On the way home I passed Hyde Park, Green Park and Kensington Gardens.
  (The list is ongoing at first but then concludes with a downward inflection), as the list is finished.
- The day was fine not rainy - contrast of ideas.
- In winter we have hot chocolate, in summer we have iced tea.

Train your ear to listen to the *implications* used in the voice to convey the meaning.

Questions

Upwards in questions which do not begin with question-words.

Examples:

- Are you going out?
- Is this your first visit?
- Will you be going today?
- Have you found the book?

Grade 5

Downwards in questions which begin with question-words.

Examples:

- Where are you going? ↘
- Which way is the exit? ↘
- What did you do yesterday? ↘
- When does the post arrive? ↘
- Why haven't you learnt your pieces? ↘

Commands and exclamations take a downward inflection

Examples:

- Get Out! ↘
- Help! ↘

TONE

Tone is a good vocal quality or timbre. Technically we achieve a good tone to our voice (as discussed in Grade Four on breath control) when tension is eliminated from our bodies, our posture is relaxed, we have good head, neck and spine alignment, and the voice has good breath support. Therefore the resonating *spaces* in our body are fully open and the vibrating surfaces are free to direct the sound and to give each sound its full value.

Tone 'colouring' denotes the appropriate emotional quality in our voice - matched to the subject matter. It can express warmth, coldness, gentleness or tension and these emotions are conveyed *mentally*. As we cannot separate mind and body (this is one of the tenets of the Alexander Principle) an emotion conveyed mentally will be reflected in the sound of your voice.

Grade 5

To summarise

All the aspects of vocal expression mentioned feature the *use of emphasis*, giving extra *significance* to a word or phrase,

- by stress (extra breath force)
- change of pace
- change of tone
- pause - before or after a word
- change of pitch
- change of volume
- the use of gesture and facial expression, bodily expression.

The usual order of speech is - thought, eyes, facial expression, gestures and body language, speech.

Gesture and the use of bodily expression - movement and language are linked. One of the most surprising findings of research into the way people receive communication messages is that the *visual* impact of communication is more powerful than the verbal:

- 55% of the impact of the speaker on the audience is *visual*
- 38% is the *sound* of the voice
- 7% is the content - the use of words.

This information certainly colours the way we view performance. 'Voice' must be understood to be part of the whole physical performance. The impact of visual communication cannot be separated from sound and content - they are all interdependent.

Movement and gesture in drama is to be *felt* and not *imposed*. In verse and prose gestures are usually superfluous. In Public Speaking gestures should come naturally, perhaps hand gestures to illustrate something. Be aware of mannerisms though - they can be very off-putting to your audience. Eye contact is *vital*. The emphasis of a word or phrase will be more effective if accompanied by eye contact - with appropriate facial expression. This also helps your pause points.

Grade 5

Use the text to guide your choice - if your prose choice is more reflective then it would be more effective to stay in the 'world' of the piece. If the writing suggests the retelling of a story, then establish eye contact. Generally in verse we stay with the 'world' of the piece. In Drama the eyes of the performer are kept within the scene, except for asides or when the audience should participate. In Public Speaking avoiding eye contact makes you look as if you are unsure of yourself or that you don't believe in what you are saying. Facial expression must be appropriate, arise from the mood and atmosphere to be conveyed, and from emotion and characterisation.

These primitive signals of the *sound* of our voice and body language - also known as non-verbal communication - are very revealing if there is a *disparity* between the verbal and non-verbal communication - we *trust* the non-verbal signals, rather than the words used. This study of gesture and body language gives us a deeper insight into other people and therefore ultimately ourselves. This knowledge can be used to great effect in Drama, e.g. In Shakespeare's 'King Lear', when Regan and Goneril want to persuade their father (King Lear) to part with his kingdom, they use elaborate language with an appropriate tone to their voices, but their facial expressions/body language *reveal* their true feelings.

Grade 5

To Summarise the main points

- The elements of vocal variety - pitch, pace, pause, inflection, tone and power are the main facets of vocal expression which we use to help us *to be understood*. They add colour to our speech. The general rule to be applied should be that the subject matter always dictates the choice of when we use these elements of vocal expression. Notice how many of these elements are linked together; don't be tempted to learn and apply them as separate topics.

- *Pitch* - Height and depth of our voice. Three main levels - use the content of your work to guide you. We aim for variety of pitch within a piece:- accentuation, emphasis, a change of thought, an emotional involvement, characterisation.

- *Pace* - The variation of the rates used in delivery - aim for *variety* of pace to maintain interest. Please don't adopt a pace in your piece and stick to it! Notice how a fast pace is *linked* to a high pitch, and a slow pace is linked to a low pitch. Use it to emphasise words, choose a different rate from the main body of the text. Slow down to highlight names, and slow down at the end of your pieces - don't end abruptly!

- *Power* - The power of the voice is not dependent on the loudness of the voice. We can achieve impact by using a quieter voice but with greater articulation. As with pitch and pace, *power* can be used for emphasis.

Grade 5

- **Pause** - Good use of pause .....silence..... can be as *effective as good use of words*. Develop your listening skills - get used to *listening* to each other's work, observe how and *when* pause points are used. Re-create in performance an interval of time which is spontaneous in natural speech. In the examination room - *pause* after announcing the title of your pieces, wait and pause when you've finished - before rushing onto the next piece.

    Partial Pauses in prose are 'sense pauses'.
    Dramatic Pauses in drama / prose - 3 types:
    - Rhetorical - before the word you wish to emphasise - the audience must anticipate what is to follow.
    - Oratorical - after the word you are emphasising - the audience reflects on what has just been said.
    - Emotional - to indicate a chaotic state of mind - pauses placed anywhere in the sentence.

- **Inflection** - the *gentle* rise and fall of the voice on the ends of words, to suggest the *implication* in our voice - it expresses meaning, it is not used for variety or effect. We should equate the inflections in our voice with the *sub-text* of a play - what is meant behind the words actually spoken? The glides in our voice are either upwards or downwards to varying degrees - we have simple rising and falling inflections, double rising and falling, compound rising and falling inflections. A general guideline for usage is: the more inflections used in your voice the *deeper the implications* that the *words* can *convey - extra meanings* are *implied* by your *tone* of voice.

- ***Tone*** - a good vocal quality. This is achieved when the voice has good breath support, the resonating cavities are fully open and the sound is well directed to give each speech sound its full value. This requires the right relaxation, posture and appropriate frame of mind to suit the subject matter. If we are feeling despondent for instance, our body language mirrors this image - slumped chests, lowered heads, raised shoulders, clenched fists and jaws and the *sound* of our voice reveals our inner turmoil. We can define tone 'colouring' therefore as the emotional quality in our voice. Remember the mind/body unity we discussed in Grade Four - how we *feel* is reflected in our bodily image which in turn affects the *sound* of our voice.

- ***Gesture and the Use of Body Language*** - The visual impact of communication is more *powerful* than the verbal. How much we express through the *unspoken* language of the body and face. The primitive signals of the *sound* of our voice and *body language* are very revealing. If there is a *disparity* between the verbal and non-verbal communication - we *trust* the non-verbal signals rather than the words used. There is a primitive intuitive reaction to these signs and sounds and we learn to de-code the messages they are sending out. *Make use* of this knowledge in your work - be aware of the signals *you* may be sending out *inadvertently*. It may be that you *want* the audience to notice there is an *incongruity* between the words you use, your tone of voice and your bodily gestures and movements. *You* must decide because *you* have to be in control!

<u>Grade 5</u>

GRADE FIVE WRITTEN PAPER

(Other points covered in previous Grades).

Gesture and the use of bodily expression

How much we express through the *unspoken language* of the body and face! We should *equate* non-verbal communication with the *sub-text of a play* - what is going on *behind* the scenes, behind the spoken words! We convey information through conscious or *unconscious* gestures, bodily movements or facial expressions.

There are 3 main uses of body language:
- a *conscious* replacement for speech
- to *reinforce* speech
- as a *mirror* or *betrayer* of mood.

There is a primitive *intuitive* reaction to a person's body language - when the language is not *congruent*. The body's unspoken signals carry *five* times more weight than the spoken word, so when speech and body language are at odds - deceit is a possible reason.

We can use body language to look confident and receptive or defensive and insecure. When we feel at ease in a situation we tend to leave the front of our bodies more exposed. *Observe* a *cat* - when it's really happy and relaxed, it rolls on the floor offering up its underbelly for stroking! Most of us are slightly more reserved in our behaviour - but when we feel confident, we use open relaxed gestures - we don't need to protect the vulnerable parts from attack!

Make sure the *signals* you send out match what you want to display; so rather than wrapping your arms across your body and crossing your legs, a closed position which suggests you are protecting yourself as well as giving yourself reassurance, convey confidence through a more open position - erect posture, arms by your side and feet firmly on the ground. Good posture not only makes you feel better, more alert - but is vital for voice production. When we slump, others interpret this as our having a depressed, defeatist attitude.

Learn to be aware of the signals you may be inadvertently sending out. Habits are easily formed; if someone moves or talks quickly and abruptly, we can interpret this to mean they are impatient or irritated, but it could be just their *habitual* style of moving and speaking.

When we are ill at ease in a situation, many of us use body language that reflects a stress response. We show our discomfort through gestures that indicate a primitive 'fight for flight' response. Fists are clenched, jaws set, legs braced, chests puffed out - or we may constantly fidget.

An apologetic posture and incoherent mumbling causes a reaction in others - perhaps the examiner interprets these signals as a lack of preparation? How do we react to a self-important swagger and a pompous, booming voice?

We can identify at least six facial expressions found throughout the world - suggesting they are inborn rather than learned (happiness, sadness, surprise, fear, anger and disgust). These facial expressions are quite subtle and should not be super-imposed. We mustn't make the mistake of old-fashioned elocutionists who tried to categorise and impose facial expressions from the outside. Facial expression is an external expression of an internal emotion - triggered by our sensitivity to words and the emotions they convey. Interestingly, the two basic facial expressions, happiness or sadness, occur naturally in blind and deaf children.

Grade 5

Apart from the face, the most visually expressive features are the hands. *Open* hand gestures mostly show a speaker's wish for rapport with an audience, a sign of trustworthiness. Eye contact plays an important part in all kinds of relationships. Avoiding eye contact looks as if you are unsure about yourself or that you don't believe in what you are saying. Confident speakers make frequent eye contact - but make sure it is *contact* with the other person - avoid rapid up and down movements - which can make you look devious.

Enjoy observing the unspoken language of the body and face and put it to good use in creating believable characters in performance.

'Suit the action to the word, the word to the action.'
Hamlet

GRADE SIX

Candidates are asked about:
- **Vocal variety**
- **Modulation**
- **Formation of vowel sounds and consonants.**

Vocal Variety (covered in Grade Five).

Modulation
We can define modulation as our flexible vocal range and how this complements the work we are presenting or performing, to bring out the emotion of the piece. Modulation *uses* the elements of vocal expression - pitch, pace, pause, power, inflection and tone (examined in both Grades Five and Six) to help *you* create the effect *you* want to achieve, whilst respecting the writer's intentions. Remember as a performer, you are the *conduit* between the writer and the audience.

So what do we mean by a 'well-modulated' voice? - one that can be adjusted and regulated to suit the subject matter. We need to think how we can *apply* those elements of vocal variety to enhance the text and bring out the meaning of what we need to communicate. Remember, we are all individuals and each of us will use those elements of vocal variety in our own unique way. This is what makes performance so exciting!

What must we do to our voice to make sure it is well-modulated? In its literal definition, modulation means to adjust or vary the tone or pitch of the speaking voice. So, how do we achieve this? We need to re-trace our steps and consider what we have digested with regard to breath into voice and then shaped into speech; and understand the relative values of these elements which contribute to the whole. Explore your vocal range but be guided by your imagination and the text!

As we have already explained well-absorbed technique allows us to *concentrate* on what we need to express. We become *better*

Grade 6

performers because *we* are in control - the task is knowing *how* to *apply* the elements of vocal variety you have at your disposal. *Think* how you can present your material to its full advantage - you will need to *discuss* your ideas with the examiner and use examples from *your* pieces. *Enjoy* the challenge of *widening* your vocal range to complement a variety of pieces. And as success breeds success, once you feel more *confident* as a performer, you will also become an *avid* reader as you search for new pieces to perform! Performance is certainly *another way in* to discover the wealth of material that we have at our disposal, and encourages our candidates to explore the works of our dramatists, poets and novelists.

Here are two contrasting pieces as examples. I do suggest that you choose *contrasting* pieces to present at an examination, to show the extent of your ability to communicate the spoken word.

Silence - a sonnet by Thomas Hood and an extract from ***Lord of the Flies*** by William Golding.

Silence

There is a silence, where hath been no sound.
There is a silence, where no sound may be;
In the cold grave, under the deep, deep sea,
or in wide desert where no life is found,
which hath been mute, yet still sleeps profound.
No voice is hushed, no life treads silently,
but clouds and cloudy shadows wander free,
That never spoke, over the idle ground.
But in green ruins, in desolate walls
Of Ancient palaces, where man hath been,
Though the dun' fox and wild hyena calls,
and owls that flit continually between,
and Shriek to the echo, and the low winds moan.
There, the true silence is - self-conscious and alone.

First we should analyse the *construction* of the sonnet to follow the poet's thought pattern. What does the title *Silence* tell us about the content? It's a poem about *silence* - so we must *use* our voice accordingly, think about your *tone* of voice. The *pace* would be slow and deliberate at first. We should be aware, that though we would choose a low *pitch* to complement the subject matter, we do need *variety* to add interest. Don't fall into the trap of deciding an *overall* pitch and pace, and continuing with it throughout. *Listen* to the sounds in the word - **Silence** , use your *voice* to bring out the eerie haunting qualities of this word.

As the contents of this poem unfold, *use* your voice accordingly. Notice how many words are continually *repeated*; the poet is emphasising these words again and again as well as similar vowel sounds in other words e.g. silence, wide, life, idle, no, cold, spoke, deep, sleep, be, sea, free, sound, found, profound, ground.

Observe the punctuation - use this information to vary the length of the *pause* points. Look at the phrasing, the *varying* length of the phrases. Do you notice how some words are *emphasised* at these pause points in the middle of the lines? e.g. silence, grave, mute, hushed, spoke. Compare the words emphasised at the end of the line, silence - sound (this contrast of opposites is called antithesis). Use variation of *volume* to add to the poignancy of the words. Make sure the *inflections* you use don't fall into a repetitive pattern.

In line 9 the word 'But' is quite significant - the mood of the poem *changes*, notice how the poet uses language to create the effect he wants *you* to interpret. The phrases are longer and you have to react to words like 'flit', 'shriek', 'echo', 'low', 'moan', 'alone'. The language should compel you to speed up, to react to the change of thought. The last line changes again - bring out the feeling of the unnatural emptiness and desolation.

'Painting is silent poetry, poetry is eloquent painting.'
Simonides, Greek poet

Grade 6

With the next example - a powerful, menacing passage from *Lord of the Flies*, which explores the issues of disillusionment with human nature; I think it is a good idea to begin with a short introduction which puts the audience in the picture of what is happening. Don't forget to *use* the element of *surprise* to your advantage - *shock* your audience into realising that the *beast* is the boy Simon, - but don't give it away too soon!

Lord of the Flies

The circle became a horseshoe. A thing was crawling out of the forest. It came darkly, uncertainly. The shrill scream that rose before the beast was like a pain. The beast stumbled into the horseshoe.

"Kill the beast! Cut his throat! Spill his blood!"

The blue-white scar was constant, the noise unendurable. Simon was crying out something about a dead man on a hill.

"Kill the beast! Cut his throat! Spill his blood! Do him in!"

The sticks fell and the mouth of the new circle crunched and screamed. The beast was on its knees in the centre, its arms folded over its face. It was crying out against the abominable noise something about a body on the hill. The beast struggled forward, broke the ring and fell over the steep edge of the rock to the sand by the water. At once the crowd surged after it, poured down the rock, leapt on to the beast, screamed, struck, bit, tore. There were no words, and no movements but the tearing of teeth and claws.'

After reading this short passage through, I'm sure you're struck by the horror conveyed by these *words*. How potent the images are! The passage begins quietly as the scene unfolds. Look at the sentence construction, the varying length of the phrases. You are the narrator at first and then you have to suddenly interject with the wild outbursts from the group. Match your

Grade 6

vocal range to the words e.g. 'shrill screaming', pain, kill. Notice the words in italics - the exclamation marks! - try to emulate the *frenzy* of the boys - you should feel compelled to quicken the *pace*, to raise the *pitch* of your voice. Feel the terror of the "beast" - and the uncontrollable behaviour of the group - as they rip Simon apart, without any compassion for him at all. Vary the level of *volume* as you *react* to the words. *Feel* the differing *pause* points - as the scene unfolds and the images surge forward.

The irony is that the boys have become 'beasts' in the end. We need a great deal of *contrast* in this piece, so that it doesn't lose its effect. *Vary* the pace and pitch of the voice; the levels of volume and tone; use your pause points to work towards the climax and then to slow down to the ending - shocked, speechless and numb.

> *'The few really great - the major novelists ...... are significant in terms of the human awareness they promote; awareness of the possibilities of life.'*
> **F. R. Leavis, Critic**

I include some more practice pieces for you to explore. *Think* about how *you* can use all the elements of vocal variety that you have absorbed and can now employ. Go through each item of pitch, pace, pause, power, inflection and tone, and decide how your voice can bring out the many colours in our words, creating mood and atmosphere.

A passage from **The Wind in the Willows** by Kenneth Grahame brings out the sadness and pathos in the writing - as poor Mole is torn between his loyalty to Ratty and the natural beckoning of his familiar home.

Moods of Rain by Vernon Scannell - certainly everything you've learnt so far can be put to the test in this poem! See the notes on Verse pauses, covered in Grade Seven. Remember the explanations regarding Onomatopoeia, Alliteration and Assonance. Make sure you have good breath control too!

Grade 6

The Birds by Daphne du Maurier - a never-to-be forgotten film directed by Alfred Hitchcock, who captured the menacing power of the birds. Can your interpretation be as effective?

And finally, a poem that on first reading seems inadequate for a Grade Six student! Quite a challenge though to perform well; we need to develop the range of the two voices, the headmaster and boy - and the humour needs to be well pointed. A rather ironic title! - ***Conversation Piece*** by Gareth Owen - as the poem exploits the lack of communication fuelled by our misunderstanding of words.

The Wind in the Willows

'Poor Mole stood alone in the road, his heart torn asunder, and a big sob gathering, gathering, somewhere low down inside him, to leap up to the surface presently, he knew, in passionate escape. But even under such a test as this his loyalty to his friend stood firm. Never for a moment did he dream of abandoning him. Meanwhile, the wafts from his old home pleaded, whispered, conjured, and finally claimed him imperiously. He dared not tarry longer within their magic circle. With a wrench that tore his very heart-strings he set his face down the road and followed submissively in the track of the Rat, while faint, thin little smells, still dogging his retreating nose, reproached him for his new friendship and his callous forgetfulness.

With an effort he caught up the unsuspecting Rat, who began chattering cheerfully about what they would do when they got back, and how jolly a fire of logs in the parlour would be, and what a supper he meant to eat; never noticing his companion's silence and distressful state of mind. At last, however, when they had gone some considerable way further, and were passing some tree-stumps at the edge of a copse that bordered the road, he stopped and said kindly, "Look here,

Mole, old chap, you seem dead tired. No talk left in you, and your feet dragging like lead. We'll sit down here for a minute and rest. The snow has held off so far, and the best part of our journey is over."

The Mole subsided forlornly on a tree-stump and tried to control himself, for he felt it surely coming. The sob he had fought with so long refused to be beaten. Up and up, it forced its way to the air, and then another, and another, and others thick and fast; till poor Mole at last gave up the struggle, and cried freely and helplessly and openly, now that he knew it was all over and he had lost what he could hardly be said to have found.'

Moods of Rain
It can be so tedious, a bore
Telling a long dull story you have heard before
So often it is meaningless;
Yet, in another mood,
It comes swashbuckling, swishing a million foils,
Feinting at daffodils, peppering tin pails,
Pelting so fast on roof, umbrella, hood,
You hear long silk being torn;
Refurbishes old toys, and oils
Slick surfaces that gleam as if unworn.
Sometimes a cordial summer rain will fall
And string on railings delicate small bells;
Soundless as seeds on soil
Make green ghosts rise.
It can be fierce, hissing like blazing thorns.
Or side-drums hammering at night-filled eyes
Until you wake and hear a long grief boil
And, overflowing, sluice
The lost raft of the world.
Yet it can come as lenitive and calm
As comfort from the mother of us all
Sighing you into sleep
Where peace prevails and only soft rain falls.

Grade 6

The Birds

They waited. The kitchen clock struck seven. There was no sound. No chimes, no music. They waited until a quarter past, switching to the Light. The result was the same. No news bulletin came through.

'We've heard wrong,' he said, 'they won't be broadcasting until eight o'clock.' They left it switched on, and Nat thought of the battery, wondered how much power was left in it. It was generally recharged when his wife went shopping in the town. If the battery failed they would not hear the instructions.

'It's getting light,' whispered his wife, 'I can't see it, but I can feel it. And the birds aren't hammering so loud.'

She was right. The rasping, tearing sound grew fainter every moment. So did the shuffling, the jostling for place upon the step, upon the sills. The tide was on the turn. By eight there was no sound at all. Only the wind. The children, lulled at last by the stillness, fell asleep. At half past eight Nat switched the wireless off.

'What are you doing? We'll miss the news,' said his wife.

'There isn't going to be any news,' said Nat. 'We've got to depend upon ourselves.'

I have purposely made only general suggestions on how to perform these pieces. The old elocutionists were stifled by rigid rules. Pieces were heavily marked with pause points and inflections, which hampered the students ability to develop a sensitive, individual performance and most importantly to *think for themselves*!

Grade 6

Conversation piece

Late again Blenkinsop?
What's the excuse this time?
Not my fault sir.
Who's fault is it then?
Grandma's sir.
Grandma's. What did she do?
She died sir.
Died?
She's seriously dead all right sir.
That makes four grandmothers this term.
And all on P.E. days Blenkinsop.
I know. It's very upsetting sir.
How many grandmothers have you got Blenkinsop?
Grandmothers sir? None sir.
None?
All dead sir.
And what about yesterday Blenkinsop?
What about yesterday sir?
You missed maths.
That was the dentist sir.
The dentist died?
No sir. My teeth sir.
You missed the test Blenkinsop.
I'd been looking forward to it too sir.
Right, line up for P.E.
Can't sir.
No such word as can't. Why can't you?
No kit sir.
Where is it?
Home sir.
What's it doing at home?
Not ironed sir.
Couldn't you iron it?
Can't do it sir.
Why not?
My hand sir.
Who usually does it?
Grandma sir.
Why couldn't she do it?
Dead sir.

Grade 6

- **Formation of vowel sounds and consonants**

In Grade One you learnt that the organs of speech are the tongue, teeth, lips, hard and soft palate. We must now add a little more detail for you to understand how vowel and consonant sounds are made, before we can explain how to correct them in Grade Seven.

1. Lips.
2. Teeth.
3. Alveolar Ridge.
4. Hard Palate.
5. Soft Palate
6. Uvula.
7. Tip of Blade of Tongue.
8. Front of Tongue.
9. Centre of Tongue.
10. Back of Tongue.

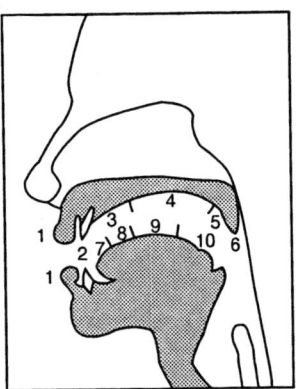

The breath starts the sound by striking the vocal cords when they are 'approximated', causing them to vibrate and set up sound waves. The initial sound is then *amplified* and *resonated* through the body - formed into words by the movement or articulation of the organs of speech. We have tone of *voice* - *breath* into *sound*. The correct placing and balance of vowels and consonants add another dimension of *resonance* to the voice. The *vowel* sounds are the instrument of *expression* in any word - the *tone* of our voice. By placing the *tone* forward the voice carries better. *Clarity* comes from having firm, distinct *consonants* - the framework of our speech. As each person has a different physical make-up and a different emotional response to words, every performance will be unique to that person.

Careful articulation is important because it enables you to speak with the *least* muscular effort. Notice when people are skilled in any physical activity, they have learned to use their muscles in a relaxed and efficient manner and they do not tire easily. Better muscular skill in speaking means greater *audibility*. Our listeners can then concentrate on *what* we have to *say*. It's surprising

Grade 6

though how so many people are meticulous about their appearance but have a rather casual attitude to the effect that careless, sloppy speech has and how damaging it is to their image.

- **_Formation of vowel sounds_**

To reiterate what you have learnt from Grade One:

- A vowel always has a free passage of sound through the mouth and it is always vocalised. The *different sounds* are made by the *shaping of the lips* and the position of the *tongue*. Of course we must be aware that the *freedom* of the *jaw* and the *mobility* of the *soft palate* make their own *contribution* to the *quality* of the sound.

- **_Monophthongs_**
  12 single vowel sounds in all - 7 short sounding single vowels as in

    Th<u>a</u>t b<u>oo</u>k <u>i</u>s n<u>o</u>t m<u>u</u>ch b<u>e</u>tt<u>e</u>r.

  and 5 long-sounding single vowels as in:

    W<u>e</u> d<u>o</u> f<u>a</u>r m<u>o</u>re w<u>o</u>rk!

  We call these sounds 'pure' vowel sounds as the shape is *complete* and *unaltered* as we say them.

- **_Diphthongs_**
  Two monophthongs glided together and spoken in the space of time it takes to speak one sound. The shape changes as you speak, with the *stress* on the first vowel sound as it glides into the second sound.

  Incidentally, diphthongs are where we get the *variations* in our regional speech - as one sound glides into the other. As we all have different conceptions of what the vowels should *sound* like, you should become aware of the *feel* of sounds in

Grade 6

your mouth, as well as observing yourself in a mirror. An effective exercise is to *mouth* a piece of text, without sound, to *feel* the different muscular movements. Repeat, separating the vowels from the consonants and listen to the startling effect! For classification purposes we use Standard English (Received Pronunciation) as a 'model' to base our work on - but as a Board we accept work in a variety of accents, provided speech is clear, easy to understand and is *appropriate* to the work being presented.

There are 8 diphthongs in all, 5 **'falling'** - literally the weight of your voice falling from the first vowel gliding into the second vowel sound, as in: **mice don't make loud noises**.

You should know which two monophthongs form the diphthongs. We'll use the above sentence as our model.

mice, **'i'** in 'mice' is made up of the vowel sounds heard in the words 'had' and 'hid'.

don't, **'oh'** in 'don't' is made up of the vowel sounds heard in the words 'the' and 'put'.

make, **'ay'** in 'make' is made up of the vowel sounds heard in the words 'pet' and 'pit'.

loud, **'ow'** in 'loud' is made up of the vowel sounds heard in the words 'had' and 'put'.

noises, **'oy'** in 'noises' is made up of the vowel sounds heard in the words 'saw' and 'hid'.

Grade 6

The three 'centring' diphthongs end in the neutral vowel sound (the sound contained in the word th*e*) as in: 'th*e* table is laid'.

p**ie**r is made up of the vowel sounds heard in the words 'pit' and 'the'.

p**ai**r is made up of the vowel sounds heard in the words 'pet' and 'the'.

p**oo**r is made up of the vowel sounds heard in the words 'put' and 'the'.

For Grade Six we add another five vowel *glides* to the 20 vowel sounds learnt in Grade One.

- **Triphthongs**
  These are formed by using the 5 'falling' diphthongs with the addition of the neutral vowel at the end of the glide, therefore making 3 shapes to the mouth!

m**i**ce & th**e**	as in the words - admire, fire, buyer, liar, diary.
d**o**n't & th**e**	as in the words slower, grower, lower.
m**a**ke & th**e**	as in the words player, prayer, layer.
l**ou**d & th**e**	as in the words our, hour, flower, flour, coward, shower.
n**oi**ses & th**e**	as in the words royal, employer, lawyer.

The weight of your voice falls from the first vowel of the diphthong to the second vowel sound and *glides* into the neutral vowel. For Received Pronunciation - you need to make sure you don't make two syllables out of the sounds! Although these sounds are not as prevalent as they were twenty years ago, it is important that you know how they are formed and can use them in performance, when you need to.

When following through the vowel sequence, remember to keep the *tongue* tip down behind the bottom front teeth.

Grade 6

Relax the jaw, which should have a thumb-width opening. With the *lip* vowels the shape of the lips varies from a small opening to being quite open. Never extend the lips beyond your natural shape. We call this a 'neutral' shape, otherwise the sound is distorted, - think about keeping the tone *forward* in the mouth not back in the throat. Lip movements need to be fluid - make sure you move the top lip too! Aim for a flexible jaw, although only the bottom hinge of the jaw is able to move. It's essential to keep the head and neck free of tension. Don't be tempted to *push* with the *head* - as if helping to push the sounds out - as this makes the neck tight and closes the throat, which in turn tenses the back of the tongue and soft palate, closing off the resonance from the chest and the throat (pharynx).

As we have already established, the *breath* is the *initial* impulse; the breath starts the sound by striking the vocal cords when they are 'approximated', that is when they are drawn together, causing them to vibrate and so set up sound waves. The initial sound is then *amplified* and *resonated* through the main cavities (throat, head) with secondary vibrations from the chest and the bones in the head (sinuses). This *sound* can be formed into words by the articulation of the organs of speech (tongue, teeth, lips, hard and soft palates).

We have to link *vocal energy* with the *muscular energy* needed to define our words, and so we need to exercise the muscles we use to make vowels and consonants, to keep them agile.

When exercising, we need to feel a sense of relaxation and freedom in the head, neck, shoulders and to keep the tone *forward* in the mouth, especially for the vowel sounds. The most important part of this section on vowel formation is the series of *exercises*, you must *feel* the sensation of throwing the sounds forward and use a hand mirror to see what is happening.

Grade 6

- **Jaw**
  Unclench your teeth! - keep the jaw open - develop this as a regular exercise, which can be done at various times during the day. You'll be amazed how we manage to get into a habit of tense, rigid jaws!

- **Tongue Tip**
  Put one finger on each corner of your mouth, to keep your jaw open, and let your tongue tip tap the alveolar ridge - lah lah lah - tap slowly, feel the pressure of the tongue tip against the ridge behind the teeth - yet *not* touching the teeth. The back of the tongue should be free and the throat open.

  With the tip behind the teeth ridge and the side of the tongue firmly against the top gums say - tah, tah, tah - tap the tongue tip *slowly*, so that you feel the *contact* between the tongue and the alveolar ridge.

  With the same position - say 'dah dah dah' - hold the pressure and feel the *vibration* between the tongue and the ridge - as this is a *voiced* sound. The vibration will be quite positive as you release it - so you'll know where the sound is placed.

  Repeat with 'n' - nah nah nah - For this consonant, the soft palate is lowered to allow the sound to escape through the nose. Hold the sound, feel the position of the tongue and the *vibration* on the tongue-tip and *resonance* in the nose. It is important to feel the tongue as firm as for 'd' - otherwise the nasal resonance will continue into the vowel. Alternate dah nah, dah nah. Release the vowel in n-ah through the mouth and not partially through the nose.

- **Back of the Tongue**
  Exercising the back of the tongue is *vital* for clarity of diction - if the back of the tongue is slack it makes the tone and speech muffled and difficult to get forward. We need to

Grade 6

become aware of the soft palate - if there is tension in the back of the soft palate the tone is metallic.

Press the back of the tongue up against the soft palate, which lowers to meet it, and notice the pressure:-

say	:	kah - throw the sound forward,
then	:	gah
alternate with	:	ke ke ke - feel the different pressures
and	:	ge ge ge
and finally	:	ng - ah. (use a hand mirror to see the movement of the soft palate).

- **The Lips**
  Press the lips firmly together.

Say	:	pah pah pah
	:	bah bah bah

You really *feel* the sound going forward - you *want* to share what you have to say! Immobile lips give the impression of a reluctance to speak.

m - is a nasal consonant, so the soft palate is lowered, yet the sound must be firm and the vowel clear of nasality - *m*ah - hold the sound before releasing it into the vowel, feel its vibration (your lips should tickle).

* For *all* sounds, other than the nasal consonants - m, n, ng, - the soft palate is *raised* to prevent the passage of air down the nose.

Exercise rounding lips from open position to a rounded one:

        AH   OO

then AH   AW   OO

Grade 6

Feel the tone *forward* on the lips for each sound, then add OH - exaggerate the two movements of this diphthong:

    AH   AW   OH   OO

We'll put the vowel and the consonants together, press the lips firmly together:

    MAH MAW MOH MOO. ***Repeat with*** P and B.

    L } tap the tongue tip firmly on the
    N } alveolar ridge

We must aim for agile speech organs - to place the tone forward. This is very important for the vowel sounds as *accuracy* depends on the *ear*. Remember to keep the tongue tip down as you glide into the vowel sound and a thumb width jaw opening!

We'll concentrate on the lip diphthongs:

    OH   OW   OI

Exaggerate the two shapes of the lips, keep the tongue free otherwise it can alter the sound, then add:

    M in front of the vowels
    MOH   MOW   MOI, ***repeat with*** P and B.

Make sure your lips don't spread *beyond* their natural position when sounding the vowels, don't force the lips into a smile, it encourages the vowel sound to go *back* in the mouth.

Grade 6

Now for the **_Tongue Vowels_**.

We move from AH - tongue in a flat position to EE - tongue in a highly arched forward position. Keep the *tip* of the tongue down, exercise the *blade* of the tongue:

      AH   AY (diphthong)   EE   I (diphthong)

With the diphthongs you should feel the blade of the tongue move considerably - watch yourself in a mirror!

Add the consonants

      L   LAH LAY LEE LIE. ***Repeat with*** T, D and N.

With AIR and EAR we should feel and see movement at the front part of the blade of the tongue - the tongue starts in a high arched position and goes down.

      L   LAIR LEAR. ***Repeat with*** T, D and N

The tongue tip consonants assist in keeping the vowel sounds forward.

Now go through the sequence of the vowel sounds - the 25 vowels in Standard English (Received Pronunciation)

The Lip Vowels

OO	as in	lose	
oo	as in	look	
OH	as in	go	(diphthong)
OH-er	as in	slower	(triphthong)
AW	as in	law	
OOR	as in	pure	(diphthong)
o	as in	lot	
OW	as in	house	(diphthong)
OW-er	as in	flower	(triphthong)
OI	as in	boy	(diphthong)
OI-er	as in	lawyer	(triphthong)

Grade 6

To the *Tongue Vowels*

AH	as in	lark	
u	as in	luck	
ER	as in	learn	
er	as in	father	(neutral)
a	as in	lad	
e	as in	let	
AY	as in	hay	(diphthong)
AY-er	as in	layer	(triphthong)
i	as in	link	
EE	as in	leave	
I	as in	sky	(diphthong)
I-er	as in	fire	(triphthong)
EAR	as in	ear	(diphthong)
AIR	as in	hair	(diphthong)

Now add successively to each vowel, the consonants P, B, M, L, N (which help keep the tone forward) - pay special attention to the two movements of the *diphthongs* and the three movements of the *triphthongs*. The position of the vowels must be *understood* to give the right placing, (when exercising them in isolation), but remember, in normal speech they are always in the context of a word, going *to* or coming *from* a consonant, which modifies their position.

To hear exactly what difference the correct placing of these vowels make to the tone, try sounding them with the jaw closed, when the tongue can make very little movement. Can you hear that the *tone* stays in the *back* of the mouth? A tight throat can cause a glottal attack: a spasm in the glottis that obstructs the sound. The short monophthongs are prone to glottal attack as we try to push the short sounds out. Think about keeping the throat open as you sound the vowels - nod the head gently to relax the neck. Interestingly the vowel sounds classified as Standard English (Received Pronunciation) *ensure* that each sound is given its *optimum resonance*.

Consonants at the beginning of words have more of an impetus than at the end - they also require more breath. Become aware

Grade 6

of the different sensation of the unvoiced / aspirate consonant and the voiced / vocal ones. Practice the tip of the tongue consonants and vowels -

    TOO TOH TAW TAH TAY TEE

Add D and N

Lip consonants and vowels:

    POO POH PAW PAH PAY PEE

Add B and M

Back of tongue consonants and vowels:

    KOO KOH KAW KAH KAY KEE

Add G.
Repeat with F, V, S, Z, th (voiced), th (unvoiced).

Consonants at the end of the vowel, take longer to say:

    OOT OHT AWT AHT AYT EET
    (aspirate sound)

    OOD OHD AWD AHD AYD EED
    (voiced)

There is a difference in the length of a consonant at the *beginning* or *end* of a word or syllable, and also whether it is *voiced* or *unvoiced*, *plosive* or *sustained* - which affects the length of the vowel. A *voiced* consonant takes longer to say than a unvoiced one.

Grade 6

for example 'd' takes longer than 't'
            'g'   "   'k'
            't'   "   'p'
            'z'   "   's'
            'v'   "   'f'
            'th' (this)   "   'th' (that)

Listen to how the vowel length changes - compare:

        sat   with   sad
        rate   with   raid
        feet   with   feed

Sustained consonants take longer to say than plosive consonants - compare:

        leek   with   leaf
        lead   with   leave
        fit   with   fill
        caught with   call
        lad   with   lamb

Use the examples we have explored to enhance your work, and make the words more colourful and effective.

Compare: set   -said   -self   -selves
               hat   -had   -hand   -hands
               heart -hard   -harm   -harms

I hope this has given you more of an insight into how a writer chooses words: for their rhythms as well as their meanings.

Grade 6

Classification of vowels (at-a-glance reference chart)
(CAPITALS = long sound, lower case = short sound.)

* For all vowel sounds, have a thumb-width opening of the jaw, tongue tip held down behind bottom teeth.

Monophthongs shaped predominantly by the ***LIPS*** - with the lip vowels the shape of the lip varies from being very closed circle to open. One constant sound is formed with no change of lip or tongue movement - the lips need to round but the back of the tongue must be *relaxed*, otherwise the sound will alter. The 12 'pure' vowel sounds must be correctly placed, otherwise there will be distortion to the sound of diphthongs and triphthongs.

OO	as in 'lose'	lips forward in a small firm circle, back of the tongue is raised.
oo	as in 'look'	lips in soft circle, back of tongue is raised.
AW	as in 'law'	lips forward in a soft circle, back of the tongue is raised.
o	as in 'lot'	lips fully open, back of the tongue is flat.

Monophthongs shaped predominantly by the ***TONGUE*** - where it goes from a flat position, 'AH', gradually arching upwards, so that EE is very arched in the front of the mouth.

AH	as in 'lark'	the most open vowel sound - tongue flat, mouth neutral and open.
u	as in 'luck'	lips neutral and open, centre of the tongue slightly raised.
ER	as in 'learn'	lips neutral, centre of the tongue is raised.
er	as in 'father'	lips neutral, centre of the tongue lower than 'er'.
a	as in 'lad'	lips in soft neutral circle, tongue not as high as in 'e'.
e	as in 'let'	lips in soft neutral circle, tongue further away from the palate than 'i'.
i	as in 'link'	neutral lips, the arch of the tongue not as high as for EE.
EE	as in 'leave'	neutral lips, body of the tongue high in the mouth.

Grade 6

Diphthongs - **lip sounds**. Two shapes to the mouth, made up of two monophthongs gliding together - the stress falls on the first part of the glide.

OH	as in	go
OW	as in	house
OI	as in	boy
OOR	as in	pure

Diphthongs - **tongue sounds**

AY	as in	hay
I	as in	sky
AIR	as in	hair
EAR	as in	ear

Triphthongs - **lip sounds** - 3 shapes to the mouth, neutral vowel added to the 5 falling diphthongs.

OH-er	as in	slower
OW-er	as in	flower
OI-er	as in	lawyer

Triphthongs - **tongue sounds**

AY-er	as in	layer
I-er	as in	fire

Grade 6

- ***Classification of consonants*** (at-a-glance reference chart)

Consonants are described according to whether they are *voiced* (vocal) / *unvoiced* (aspirate); which part of the speech mechanism is involved and how it is made; plosive / sustained and the subsequent variations on these two categories. They *sound* different and *feel* different.

Look how many sounds are classified as alveolars - an important area for the structure of English speech sounds.

(The chart follows on the next page.)

Grade 6

Classification of consonants chart

P	bi-labial, plosive, aspirate	pin, nip, rope	Lips together
B	bi-labial, plosive, voiced	bob, **bib**, ru**bb**er	Lips together
T	alveolar, plosive, aspirate	tat, tin, pottery	Tongue & Teeth Ridge
D	alveolar, plosive, voiced	day, **d**u**d**, sa**dd**est	Tongue & Teeth Ridge
K	velar, plosive, aspirate	kite, tack, act	Back of tongue & soft palate
G	velar, plosive, voiced	**g**a**g**, **g**row, da**gg**er	Back of tongue & soft palate
CH	alveolar, affricate, aspirate	chair, **ch**eese, **ch**ur**ch**	Tongue & Teeth Ridge
J	alveolar, affricate, voiced	**j**udge, **g**in, mid**g**et	Tongue & Teeth Ridge
TR	post-alveolar, fricative, aspirate	tree, trap, entrance	Tongue(hollowed) & Teeth Ridge
DR	post-alveolar, fricative, vocal	dream, drive, address	Tongue(hollowed) & Teeth Ridge
F	labio-dental, fricative, aspirate	fork, fun, enough	Teeth & lip
V	labio-dental, fricative, vocal	**v**im, **v**eal, Step**h**en	Teeth & lip

Continued on the next page

Grade 6

th	lingua-dental, fricative, aspirate	mouth, **thick**, breath	Tongue & teeth
TH	lingua-dental, fricative, voiced	there, **this**, loathe	Tongue & teeth
S	alveolar, fricative, aspirate	sat, **cease**, science	Tongue & teeth ridge
Z	alveolar, fricative, voiced	zoo, zeal, scissors	Tongue & teeth ridge
SH	post-alveolar, fricative, aspirate	shoe, **ship**, mansion	Tongue & teeth ridge
ZH	post-alveolar, fricative, voiced	vision, Jean, leisure	Tongue & teeth ridge
H	glottal, fricative, aspirate	had, has, whale	Vocal cords
M	bi-labial, nasal, sustained, voiced	meet, **mum**, lumber	Lips together
N	alveolar, nasal, sustained, voiced	now, many, funny	Tongue & teeth ridge
NG	velar, nasal, sustained, voiced	sun**g**, long, banquet	Back of tongue & soft palate
L	alveolar, lateral, sustained, voiced	lip, fall, value	Tongue & teeth ridge
R	post-alveolar, sustained, voiced	rip, road, carry	Tongue & teeth ridge
Y	lingua-palatal, semi-vowel, sustained, voiced	yes, yawn, onion	Tongue & hard palate
W	bi-labial, velar, semi-vowel, sustained, voiced	walk, **wall**, quarrel	Lips, back of tongue & soft palate

Grade 6

I shall now explain briefly about consonant sounds and then describe each sound in detail.

A Consonant

This is a sound in which the passage of air or sound is stopped (plosive), or partially stopped (sustained), by the organs of articulation. Consonants fall into 2 groups: those **voiced** - sounded (the vocal cords are approximated and vibrating), and those **unvoiced** or aspirate (made by breath), the vocal cords are not drawn together, it is breath that is released.

* We can only *resonate vocalised* sounds/these are the *vowels* and *vocal* / voiced *consonants*. We cannot resonate aspirate / unvoiced sounds.

Classification of consonants - the technical terms explained.

- **Plosives** - complete oral stoppage of breath flow by the lips, teeth, and hard palate followed by sudden release p, b, t, d, k, g.

- **Fricatives** - made by the friction of breath in a narrow opening, sound sustained, s, z, sh, zh, h, tr, dr, f, v, th, th.

- **Affricates** - combination of a *plosive* with an immediately following *fricative* e.g. ch in (ch)air, j in (j)ust. The first sound isn't finished before the other one starts.

- **Nasals** - sound pronounced with the breath passing through the nose, m, n, ng - the only three sounds in the English Language which do so.

- **Lateral** - breath escapes sideways - L - the sides of the tongue are lowered to allow the sound to escape and continue out through the mouth. The sound is not completed until the tongue tip is released.

- **Semi-vowels** - w, y, mouth not completely closed - takes vowel shape. Sound released as the lips part. These two

Grade 6

sounds nearly become a vowel except for a slight interuption of sound.

- **Alveolars** - a *very important* area for *English* speech sounds, incorporating a group of alveolars known as sibilants, (because of their hissing sound), s, z, sh, zh; and post-alveolars - sounds made just behind the gum ridge, tr, dr, sh, zh, r. Sounds articulated on the hard gum ridge situated behind the top front teeth - used as a sounding board (t, d, ch, j, n, l,).

We need to strengthen the *tongue* muscle for *high* placement on the alveolar ridge, *independent* of the lower jaw. Raise the tip of the tongue to the upper teeth, keeping mouth wide open. Keep the jaw relaxed and the lips free - don't try to close the jaw in order to reach with the tongue.

Trace a small circle with your tongue, spell out names and numbers. This is a basic routine for limbering, strengthening and stretching the tongue muscle. The right pressure must be found, not *too* much as you release into the vowel, otherwise it makes the sound *hard*.

Consonants fall into 2 groups - ***plosive*** and ***sustained*** and their composite sounds.

- ***Plosives*** - p, b; t, d; k, g; ch, j - all have the passage of sound stopped for a split second by either the lips or the tongue, so that it is *held* before it is released. Air pressure builds up and it is not until the muscles *release* the air that we actually *hear* the sound. *Plosives* are paired; one unvoiced (aspirate)- the sound we hear comes out on the breath, the other *voiced* (vocal) where the vocal cords come together to make *sound*.

p & b, the lips press together to stop the air coming out, they hold the sound for a moment and when the lip muscles are released, the p & b explode out.

Grade 6

t & d, tongue tip is pressed against the alveolar ridge *behind* the teeth (keep the tongue away from the teeth) and the rims of the tongue touch the side teeth, held for a moment before being released- keep the sound light.

k & g, contact between the back of the tongue and the soft palate that forms the consonant, we hear the sound as the *tongue* is released. The soft palate is kept *raised* and only lowers for these three sounds- m, n, ng.

ch & j, closing of the jaw and the tongue pressed against the teeth and hard palate that makes the stoppage.

In all these cases, sound or air is *stopped* for a fraction of a second and when it is *released*, we then *hear* the consonant.

- ***Affricates***
  These have a *plosive* closure and a slow release with friction - combination of plosive and fricative.

  Ch, formed by the tip, blade and rims of the tongue stopping the breath flow as they meet the alveolar ridge and side teeth. At the same time the tongue is raised toward the hard palate, ready for the fricative. The plosive *t* is released slowly with friction occurring between the front regions of the tongue and the hard palate.

  J, formed in the same way as for Ch, but vocalised, starting on a *d*.

- ***Fricatives***
  Two organs of articulation are brought together close enough for the escaping air-stream to make audible friction, the sound is sustained.

  TR & DR, the centre of the tongue is hollowed ready for the R friction. The release of the stop is slow, compared with the fast plosive release of T & D and CH & J.

Grade 6

F & V, formed by top teeth making contact with bottom lip, one sound is aspirate, the other sounded.

TH & TH, teeth slightly apart, tongue *slightly* protruding out of mouth. One with voice, the other unvoiced; as in breathe, breath.

S & Z Sibilants - one with voice, the other aspirate. The tongue should seal off the escape of air along the alveolar ridge except at the very centre where a single narrow stream of air passes between the ridge and the tip of the tongue.

SH & ZH Sibilants - one with voice, the other aspirate. Formed by the sides of the tongue pressed against the gum and the blade arched high to make pressure between it and the roof of the mouth, so making friction. The jaw is almost closed, the sound is given a particular resonance by the rounding of the lips.

H, a 'glottal' fricative. It is produced by the coming together of the vocal cords and glottis (the space at the upper end of the wind pipe and between the vocal cords) to create a friction of air.

- ***Nasals***
There is a closure of two organs of articulation in the mouth, but the soft palate (velum) is *lowered*, (only for the three sounds - m, n, ng.) so air is released through the *nose*.

m, lips together, sustained sound.

n, tongue forms a closure with teeth ridge and upper side teeth as for t & d.

ng, closure is formed with the back of the tongue as for *k* and *g* but with a *lowered* soft palate. The soft palate is released, the sound vibrates in the nose - but it takes a *flexible* back of the tongue to make sure there is no audible plosion (ng-g).

Grade 6

- **Frictionless Continuants**

    A narrowing of the mouth without friction, these are termed 'continuant' because the sound will go on for as long as you can have breath!

    r, flapped r - the commonest form. Tongue tip is held near to, but not touching the upper teeth ridge. The back rims of the tongue are touching the upper molars - the central part of the tongue is lowered to produce a hollow effect. No friction and the sound escapes over the central part of the tongue. e.g. read, very, rabbit.

    l (clear), formed when the tongue tip is raised to the alveolar ridge and the sound escapes over the sides of the tongue (laterally). The *front* of the tongue is raised towards the hard palate. The clear l occurs *before* vowels. e.g. lady, million.

    l (dark), formed when the tongue tip touches the teeth ridge and the sound escapes laterally - *but* it has a back vowel quality. The *back* of the tongue is raised towards the soft palate. The dark l occurs *after* a vowel in a word and at the ends of words e.g. full, bottle.

* m, n, ng, l, r - are known as the liquid consonants, smooth-flowing and they enhance the musicality of speech.

- **Semi-vowels**

    w, y, they have vowel like qualities.

    y, this sound nearly becomes a vowel except for the slight interruption of the tongue and hard palate.

    w, formed by rounding the lips forward but the second part of the word is heard only as the lips part and release the sound in the vowel e.g. *way*.

Grade 6

Set out on below is the International Phonetic Alphabet which is readily found in modern edition dictionaries. In the Concise Oxford Dictionary (which I use) there is actually a key at the bottom of each page! This information, once thought to be the province of specialists, is now readily available to assist and benefit all those who are interested in increasing their knowledge.

The International Phonetic Alphabet (IPA) is based on Standard English. * Please note that a knowledge of IPA is *not* essential for candidates.

Consonants

b, d, f, h, l, m, n, p, r, s, t, k, v, w, and z have their usual English values. Other symbols used are:

g	(get)	tʃ	(chip)	dʒ	(jar)
x	(loch)	ŋ	(ring)	θ	(thin)
ð	(this)	ʃ	(she)	ʒ	(decision)
j	(yes)				

Vowels

monophthongs	diphthongs	triphthongs
(single vowels)	(double vowels)	(triple vowels)

short		long					
æ (cat)		ɑː (arm)		eɪ (day)		eɪə (layer)
e (bed)		iː (see)		aɪ (my)		aɪə (fire)
ə (ago)		ɔː (saw)		ɔɪ (boy)		ɔɪə (lawyer)
ɪ (sit)		ɜː (her)		əʊ (no)		əʊə (slower)
ɒ (hot)		uː (too)		aʊ (how)		aʊə (flower)
ʌ (run)				ɪə (near)		
ʊ (put)				eə (hair)		
				ʊə (poor)		

Grade 6

To Summarise the main points

- **Vocal Variety** - we have six main facets of vocal expression; pitch, pace, pause, power, inflection and tone, to add *colour* to our speech.

- **Modulation** is the *flexible* vocal range suited to the subject matter. We *use* the elements of vocal expression to enhance our work.

- **Formation of vowels and consonants:**
  Speech Training encourages our students to *think*. Once we understand *how* sounds are formed and words are made up - we give more *thought* to the words *we* use - and the words a writer uses - which gives us a greater understanding of human nature and our need to communicate. You may be interested to know that we can think seven times faster than we can speak!

- *'Language is a form of human reason.'*
  Claude Levi-Strauss

- **Figures of Speech** - used to add emphasis and intensity to words as they achieve effects *beyond* the range of *literal* language. There is a conscious deviation on the writer's part. We react to these effects, which stimulate our imagination.

Grade 6

GRADE SIX (WRITTEN)

All aspects covered in previous Grades except Figures of Speech.

FIGURES OF SPEECH - the devices of figurative language.

Techniques for comparing dissimilar objects to achieve effects *beyond* the range of *literal* language. These effects use *emphasis* to add *intensity* to the words. This emphasis is accomplished by the user's conscious deviation from the literal sense of a word or commonly accepted word order or sentence construction (T.S. Eliot and Ezra Pound in particular used this to great advantage in their work).

Here's a sample selection of the most common ones that you need to know for this Grade, followed by a small selection of less common ones, which you will find useful for reference.

Essential Definitions

- **Allegory**
  Allegory is a story or narrative which carries an extra meaning, as well as that of its surface story or content. It is a method of telling one story whilst seeming to tell another. *The Pilgrim's Progress* (1684) by John Bunyan is one of the most famous prose allegories. As with many of its kind, it personifies abstract ideas and human virtues and vices in characters such as Mr Wordly-Wise, Giant Despair, Hopeful, Lechery, Pride and Christian, the pilgrim. Allegory and satire sometimes go hand in hand: George Orwell's novel *Animal Farm* (1945) is a good example of this.

Grade 6

- **_Alliteration_**
  Alliteration is the repetition of the same consonant sound at the beginning of a word. The listener enjoys the pattern of the sound which impress themselves upon the mind. Here is an example from Coleridge's *Kubla Khan*:

  Five <u>m</u>iles <u>m</u>eandering with a <u>m</u>azy <u>m</u>otion.

- **_Ambiguity_**
  Language with a doubtful meaning, or with several meanings - where an author *deliberately* suggests several layers of meaning. Verbal nuance, which gives room for alternative reactions to the same piece of language - which is amongst the roots of poetry.

- **_Assonance_**
  The repetition of vowel sounds in words to achieve a particular effect. In the following lines from Tennyson's *Lotus-eaters* - a drowsy, flowing rhythm is achieved by the long vowel sounds.

  'The Lotus blooms below the barren peak:
  The Lotus blows by every winding creek.
  All day the wind breathes low with mellower tone
  Thro' every hollow cave and alley lone,
  Round and round the spicy downs the yellow lotus dust is blown.'

- **_Analogy_**
  The resemblance between two different things. Sometimes expressed as a simile, e.g.

  'Tis with our judgements as our watches, none
  Go just alike, yet each believes his own.'
  Pope, An Essay on Criticism

Grade 6

- **Antithesis**
  Contrasting ideas sharpened by the use of opposite or noticeably different meanings. Here's an example from Pope's *Moral Essays*:

  'Less wit than mimic, more wit than wise.'

- **Cliché**
  A phrase or idea that has been used so often, is so well known that it has lost its original appeal, e.g. *to turn over* a new leaf.

- **Consonance**
  The close repetition of identical consonant sounds before and after different vowels:

  'flip - flop', 'creak - croak'.

- **Dissonance**
  A harsh, discordant mixture of sounds to create a particular effect - a very common device used in much poetry, e.g. Tennyson's ***Morte d'Arthur***:

  'Dry clashed his harness in the icy caves
  And barren chasms, and all to left and right
  The bare black cliff clanged around him, as he banged
  His feet on juts of slippery crag that rang
  Sharp - smitten with the dint of armed heels.'

- **Hyperbole**
  Gross exaggeration for emphasis:

  'I've told you a *million* times.'

  Andrew Marvell in *To His Coy Mistress* uses hyperbole to great effect.

Grade 6

- *Irony*
  Saying one thing whilst meaning another. Irony occurs when a word or phrase has one surface meaning, but another contradictory meaning beneath the surface. Jane Austen (1775-1817), novelist, is a master of irony:

  'Mr Collins had only to change from Jane to Elizabeth - and it was soon done - done while Mrs Bennett was stirring the fire.'
  from Pride and Prejudice

- *Malapropism*
  The muddled use of long or complex words in the wrong place or context. The term is derived from Mrs Malaprop, a character in The Rivals (1775) by Sheridan:

  'She's as headstrong as an allegory on the banks of the Nile.'

- *Metaphor*
  A comparison between two objects for the purpose of describing one of them. A metaphor states that one object is another, for example Keats refers to a vase and the decoration on it as 'Thou still unravish'd bride of quietness.' The comparison of a vase to a bride is made more forceful by the use of Metaphor. Also:

  'Life's but a walking shadow.'

  'the trains' long cries are swallowed in the throats of tunnels.'

- *Onomatopoeia*
  A word which sounds like the noise it describes, such as 'splash' or 'thwack'.

Grade 6

- **Paradox**
A statement which, though it appears self-contradictory, contains a basis of truth which reconciles the seeming opposites. A paradox concentrates the reader's attention to what is being said:

   'One short sleepe past, we wake eternally,
   And death shall be no more, Death thou shalt die.'
   from John Donne's Holy Sonnets

- **Parody**
A work written in imitation of another's work, usually with the object of making fun of or ridiculing the original, using more or less the same technique as the cartoon caricaturists. A kind of satirical mimicry. Max Beerbohn's collection of his own parodies in *A Christmas Garland* (1912) includes pieces in the manner of Kipling, Galsworthy and Hardy.

- **Personification**
The giving of human/animal qualities to inanimate objects or abstract ideas, e. g.

   The sea is a hungry dog.
   James Reeves, The Sea

- **Pun**
Word play involving the use of a word with two different meanings or two words pronounced and spelt the same way but containing different meanings.

   In John Donne's *Hymn to God the Father* the word *done* is a pun on Donne's own name, as well as the pun on *son* meaning both *Christ* and the *sun*. James Joyce made extensive use of puns in both *Ulysses* and *Finnegan's Wake*.

<u>*Grade 6*</u>

- *Simile*
A comparison between two objects where one object is said to be *like* or *as* another.

> *'The wolf with its belly stitched full of big pebbles;*
> *Nibelung wolves barbed like black pine forest*
> *Against a red sky, over blue snow.'*
> **Ted Hughes, February**

<u>**Non-Essential Definitions**</u> - but useful to know!

- *Burlesque*
A work designed to ridicule attitudes, style or subject matter - by either handling an elevated subject in a trivial manner or a low subject with mock dignity (see Parody - a close related Genre).

- *Conceit*
An elaborate and startling comparison between apparently dissimilar objects, associated in particular with Metaphysical Poetry. John Donne (1572 - 1631) compares his lover and himself to a flea (the flea has sucked the blood of both and by carrying their mixed blood in his body becomes a symbol of unity).

- *Epigram*
A short, usually witty, statement:

> *'Man is a rational animal who always loses his temper when he is called upon to act in accordance with the dictates of reason.'*

- *Euphemism*
A pleasant way to say something unpleasant - "passed away" for dying. Used to avoid offending someone through bluntness.

Grade 6

- **Litotes**
  A figure of speech which contains an understatement for emphasis - therefore the opposite of hyperbole:

  'not bad' meaning ' very good'.

- **Metonymy**
  A figure of speech in which the name of an attribute is substituted for the thing itself. e.g. *'The stage'* for the theatrical profession. *'The crown'* for the monarchy. *'The bench'* for the judiciary.

- **Oxymoron**
  A figure of speech in which words of opposite meaning are joined together, as in 'a damned saint', 'conspicuous by his absence'.

- **Synecdoche**
  A figure of speech in which a part represents the whole object or idea.

  'Give us this day our daily bread' - bread meaning meals taken each day.

GRADE SEVEN

Candidates are asked about:

- **Verse Pauses.**
- **Rhythm and Metre in Prose and Verse.**
- **Common speech faults and their correction.**

Verse Pauses

We discussed the value of Pause in Grades 5 and 6. A Pause draws attention to a word or phrase - it is used for *emphasis*. Good use of pause ..... *silence* .... can be as effective as good use of words. Attune your ears to the varying lengths of pauses and their effects. Both Samuel Beckett and Harold Pinter have exploited the value of silence in their playwriting (Theatre of the Absurd).

A *verse* pause is a pause used to separate verses or stanzas when the poet has finished a particular train of thought. Most candidates tend to forget to pause *long enough* between separate verses. e.g. in *Piano* by D. H. Lawrence, which we will use as our example (see overleaf), you need to pause between verses (stanzas) 2 and 3. Key words are *'in spite of myself'* - to indicate a new direction of thought, and *'so now'*. You need to pause to give time for the listener to appreciate the change of thought. Don't rush on! Compare this with a new paragraph in a piece of prose, lift your voice at the beginning of each verse.

Suspensory or suspensive pauses

These come at the *end* of run-on or enjambed lines in verse where the sense is *not* complete - and flows on to the next line. The voice is 'suspended' on the held, final word (which emphasises the word) at the line end, but the tone is carried onto the next line and the pause taken when the phrase is completed. These are partial pauses (no breath taken), like the sense pauses in prose - taken at the end of a phrase.

<u>*Grade 7*</u>

Shakespeare uses this to great advantage in his plays and poems placing a specially significant word at the end of the line. In *Julius Caesar*, Brutus' wife Portia uses emotional blackmail to try to persuade her husband to reveal his secret thoughts and worries:

> '..........dwell I but in the *suburbs*
> of your good pleasure?'

The voice lingers on 'suburbs' which throws it into emphasis.

In *King Lear*, Regan displays her contempt for Gloucester, after he has been blinded. The word '*smell*' emphasises that Gloucester has been reduced to the level of a beast in her eyes:

> 'Go, thrust him out at gates, and let him *smell*
> his way to Dover.'

Piano by D H Lawrence
(the suspensory pause is shown as *(sp)* followed by an arrow leading to the next line)

> Softly, in the dusk, a woman is singing to me;
> Taking me back down the vista of years, till I see *(sp)*
> ↪ A child sitting under the piano, in the boom of the tingling
>   strings
> And pressing the small, poised feet of a mother who smiles as
>   she sings.
>
> In spite of myself, the insidious mastery of *song (sp)*
> ↪ Betrays me back, till the heart of me weeps to *belong (sp)*
> ↪ To the old Sunday evenings at home, with winter *outside (sp)*
> ↪ And hymns in the cosy parlour, the tinkling piano our guide.
>
> So now it is vain for the singer to burst into *clamour (sp)*
> ↪ With the great black piano appassionato. The *glamour (sp)*
> ↪ Of childish days is upon me, my manhood is *cast (sp)*
> ↪ Down in the flood of remembrance, I weep like a child for the
>   past.

Grade 7

Metrical Pause
The lines of the verse are sometimes of an irregular length, in an otherwise regular passage. To keep the overall *shape* of the poem, metrical pauses are used. These pauses are usually partial pauses, and *stretch* certain words in the shorter lines - so that the overall duration for each line becomes almost the same. There is always a *reason* for the missing beat, a *reason* for *silence*.

In ***Othello's*** 'O, blood, blood, blood' there are three stressed beats instead of five in a line of iambic pentameter u - / u - / u - / u - / u - /

and in ***King Lear***

>'......but they shall be
>The terrors of the earth. You think I'll weep.
>No, I'll not weep.   (metrical pause)
>I have full cause of weeping;
>   but this heart   (metrical pause)
>Shall break into a hundred thousand flaws.'

When speaking blank verse, suspensive, caesural and metrical pauses are very important to the rhythmical impulse, shape and flow.

Caesural Pause (derived from the Latin, means 'a cutting')
A caesural pause is placed at some point in the line or verse. It usually occurs *after* the main word to be emphasised - no breath needs to be taken at this pause - the commonest point is in the middle of a line of verse. A line may have more than one caesura or none at all. It is often marked by punctuation.

Grade 7

i.e. - from *Sailing to Byzantium* by Yeats; - I've marked the caesural pauses (/).

> 'That is no country for old men. / the young
> In one another's arms, / birds in the trees
> - Those dying generations - / at their song,
> The salmon-falls / the mackerel-crowded seas,
> Fish, flesh, or fowl, / commend all summer long
> Whatever is begotten, / born / and dies,
> Caught in that sensual music / all neglect
> Monuments of unageing intellect.'

- ***Rhythm and Metre in Prose and Verse***
(Rhythm is derived from the Greek word 'flowing')

In *verse* or *prose* rhythm is the movement or sense of movement communicated by the arrangement of stressed and unstressed syllables and the duration of the syllables (long or short) in words and phrases.

In *verse* - the rhythm depends on the metrical pattern, the rhythm is regular. In prose it does not have to be regular. In *prose* it is the effect of the arrangement of words, length of phrases, syllables - a writer arranges his rhythms so that they intensify the expression of what is said. We have already discussed in earlier Grades, the devices a writer can use for effect, assonance, alliteration, onomatopoeia, accentuation. Note that all *stressed* syllables are *not* necessarily of the same length, nor are all short or long syllables of equal length.

Metre: means measure, a regular pattern, one that we can *anticipate*, determined by the number and length of feet in a line.

Foot: in prosody: a group of syllables constituting a metrical unit, a unit of rhythm - determined by the syllable variation.

Prosody: laws of metre and the study of speech rhythms in verse.

Grade 7

Verse: a metrical composition - opposite to *Prose* in accordance with the rules of prosody.

"A dance is a measured pace as a verse is a measured speech."
Francis Bacon

In ***rhythm***, sounds of words are skilfully arranged. A writer pays attention to the arrangement of stressed syllables, the length of these stressed syllables, which help determine the rhythm. A writer is attuned to the rhythm in words, provided by long / short vowels, the effect of plosive consonants contrasted with sustained consonants, and appreciating the difference between vocal / aspirate consonants.

Mono-syllabic words can create an atmosphere of fear, like the regular, recurring beat of your heart. We have to use our senses to direct our imagination - 'stone', 'jag', 'knife' - hard, sharp words whereas 'flowing', 'ripple', 'shimmer', are soft fluid words - because of their composite sounds we can categorise words into positive and negative.

Rhythm suggests movement and flow, giving all the sounds in speech their correct value and accentuation. Rhythm also depends on the rate of speech, the duration of the individual sounds, length of the phrases used and the duration of the pauses between phrases.

Coleridge said that the form of a successful work of art is:

'shaped from within not imposed from without'

Here is another passage from ***Lord of the Flies*** by **William Golding** - immediately following on from the passage used in Grade 6. The rhythm in this piece of prose changes from the frenetic atmosphere we observed in the previous passage - to one of resignation as the realisation that Simon is dead.

Grade 7

'Along the shoreward edge of the shallows the advancing clearness was full of strange, moonbeam-bodied creatures with fiery eyes. Here and there a larger pebble clung to its own air and was covered with a coat of pearls. The tide swelled in over the rain-pitted sand and smoothed everything with a layer of silver. Now it touched the first of the stains that seeped from the broken body and the creatures made a moving patch of light as they gathered at the edge. The water rose further and dressed Simon's coarse hair with brightness. The line of his cheek silvered and the turn of his shoulder became sculptured marble. The strange, attendant creatures, with their fiery eyes and trailing vapours, busied themselves round his head. The body lifted a fraction of an inch from the sand and a bubble of air escaped from the mouth with a wet plop. Then it turned gently in the water.

Somewhere over the darkened curve of the world the sun and moon were pulling; and the film of water on the earth planet was held, bulging slightly on one side while the solid core turned. The great wave of the tide moved further along the island and the water lifted. Softly, surrounded by a fringe of inquisitive bright creatures, itself a silver shape beneath the steadfast constellations, Simon's dead body moved out towards the open sea.'

In *poetry* there is an economy of language, heightened language containing imagery and written to be spoken aloud. *Figures of speech* are used for effect; there's a definite rhythm but that does not have to fit in with the strict grammatical structure of verse. The arrangement of words is important as well as the choice of words. Words are used for both their meaning and their sounds. We form a mental picture created by the words a writer chooses for effect. For example, in **A Poison Tree** by **William Blake**, Blake describes his anger as if it were a tree he has planted and wants to grow. **Keats** did say:

'Poetry should surprise!'

Grade 7

Faults may include the domination of *metrical stress* at the expense of *rhythmical stress* and emphasis and failure to use phrasing appropriately, so that the sound overshadows the sense. **Auden** said that poetry was :

'the delivery of passionate, memorable statements through the music of words.'

Form - is the shape and structure of a literary work and its style. The poet makes a poem or verse out of words and expresses these words, for example, in the sonnet form. We are unable to convey the feeling of the poem or verse without understanding its internal structure, its form. You should ask yourself, why the poet chose the particular *type* of verse you are reciting; narrative, lyrical, epic, ode, elegy, sonnet, ballad and how does its distinct *form* direct your performance?

Style - how a writer says things - his characteristic manner of expression in verse, prose or drama. We need to examine a writer's choice of words, his figures of speech, the shape of his sentences and paragraphs. Note how he uses language to create the effect he wants you to interpret. We can sum up by saying 'style' is the tone and 'voice' of the writer.

'Style is the man.'
Comte de Buffon, 1753

Free Verse - commonly employed in the 17th century - it abandoned certain traditional principles - especially the rules which prescribed recurrent metrical patterns and a certain number of syllables per line. Rhythm and the division of verse into rhythmical units; was held to be the essential foundation of poetic form. This rhythm was to be personal, the particular expression of the individual poet - his own voice or tune, appropriate to the subject.

Various modern Poets - Walt Whitman, T. S. Eliot, Ezra Pound, Sylvia Plath, D. H. Lawrence and Roger McGough also use free verse extensively. In free verse there is a *rhythmical beat*,

Grade 7

determined by long / short vowels, stressed and unstressed syllables, the effect of plosive and sustained consonants, and differentiating between vocal and aspirate consonants, rather than a *metrical beat* as in verse.

Metre (from the Greek word 'measure') refers to the pattern of stressed and unstressed syllables in verse.

- **The Metres of Verse**

A sequence of stressed and unstressed syllables creates a *regular* rhythm called 'metre'. Identifying metres is called scansion. When metres are identified, the syllables in a line are divided into groups of *two* or *three*, each of which is called a *foot*.

Stressed = ▬ ; unstressed = ∪

The commonest feet in English prosody are, in the following order, *iamb, trochee, dactyl, anapaest* and *spondee*. If the stress falls on the *first* syllable of a foot, the metre is trochaic (▬∪), each foot is a *trochee*.
If the stress falls on the *second* (∪▬), the metre is iambic and each foot is called an *iamb*.

Trochaic metres can sound assertive as they start with a stress:

Blake's *The Tyger*

Tyger! Tyger! burning bright
In the forests of the night

Iambic - e.g. from **Blake's *A Poison Tree***

My foe outstretched beneath the tree.

Trochaic and *Iambic* metres are based on a *two-syllable* foot.

When a foot has three syllables, two other metres are used - the *dactylic* and the *anapaestic*. A dactyl is a variation of a trochee in that it has two unstressed syllables after the stress, ▬∪∪ and an anapaest has two unstressed syllables before the stress, ∪∪▬.

There are names for the number of feet in a line. A one foot is called monometer; two a dimeter; three a trimeter; four a tetrameter; five a pentameter; six a hexameter; seven a heptameter and eight an octameter.

Much English verse is iambic and is written in tetrameters or pentameters. One of the most popular metres in English is the rhyming iambic pentameter, known as the *Heroic measure*, there are 5 feet in a verse line, each foot consisting of 2 syllables, (10 syllables in total, in a pattern of an unstressed, stressed syllable (∪▬), please remember not all stressed syllables are of equal length).

Blank Verse is poetry written in lines of *unrhymed* iambic pentameter - the nearest rhythm to our everyday speech. The Blank Verse of Shakespeare's plays is basically in iambic pentameter, but he uses inversions, additional feet, substitutions, (trochee for an iamb) and variations - (spondee), and feminine endings - (an *extra* unstressed syllable at the end of the line, giving 11 syllables to the line). Such variations are usually the expression of deep emotions *deliberately* placed for *emphasis*. You also need to study the metrical pause - Shakespeare makes much use of it of course. He also makes much use of alliteration, assonance, antithesis and other Figures of Speech for example:

King Lear
Act 2 Scene. 4

Lear:
O, reason not the need! Our basest beggars *(11 syllables)*
Are in the poorest thing superfluous.
Allow not nature more than nature needs -
Man's life is cheap as beast's. Thou art a lady;
If only to go warm were gorgeous *(9 syllables)*
Why, nature needs not what thou gorgeous wear'st,
Which scarcely keeps thee warm. But for true need -

Grade 7

You heavens, give me that patience, patience I need! *(12 syllables)*
You see me here, you gods, a poor old man,
As full of grief as age, wretched in both;
If it be you that stirs these daughters' hearts
Against their father, fool me not so much
To bear it tamely; touch me with noble anger, *(12 syllables)*
And let not women's weapons, water drops,
Stain my man's cheeks. No, you unnatural hags,
I will have such revenges on you both
That all the world shall - I will do such things -
What they are yet I know not; but they shall be *(11 syllables)*
The terrors of the earth. You think I'll weep.
No, I'll not weep. *(4 syllables) - metrical pause*
I have full cause of weeping; *(7 syllables) - metrical pause*
    (storm and tempest)
                    but this heart *(3 syllables) - metrical pause*
Shall break into a hundred thousand flaws
Or ere I'll weep. O Fool, I shall go mad!

Ask yourself - how does the rhythm contribute to the poem or line of dialogue? Rhythms enact the thoughts and feelings of verse, so it is appropriate to ask oneself - are some rhythms *more successful* at conveying these feelings?

Iambic metres can be thoughtful and recollective, they move from unstressed to stressed syllables.

        'The picture of the mind revives again.'
                    Wordsworth, *Tintern Abbey*

Dactylic metres tend to be sad. Two unstressed syllables follow the stress to create a feeling of decline, of a falling away from certainty.

    'We that had loved him so, followed him, honoured him.'
                        Browning, *The Lost Leader*

Anapaestic metres build up emotional tension by hurrying the reader through unstressed syllables to the stressed one.

Grade 7

'The Assyrian came down like the wolf on the fold.'

Notice also the power of the monosyllables - down, wolf, fold.

To summarise the main points (regarding metre)

- Verse in English poetry is measured in *feet* (as music is measured in bars). A foot is composed of *stressed* and *unstressed* syllables.

    Disyllabic feet have 2 syllables
    Trisyllabic feet have 3 syllables

- *Disyllabic Feet*
    ∪ = unstressed ; ▬ = stressed

    Iambic ∪▬ as in despair, }   whole poems are composed
    Trochaic ▬∪ as in temple }   of these e.g. Milton's 'L'Allegro'

    Spondee ▬ ▬   }   occasional feet, we cannot
    Pyrrhic ∪∪   }   compose whole poems of
                              these.

- *Trisyllabic Feet*
    Anapaest ∪∪▬ as in serenade.
    Dactyl ▬∪∪ as in willingly.

    Amphibrach ∪▬∪   }   occasional feet.
    Amphimacer ▬∪▬   }

- The commonest measure is Iambic metre, particularly Iambic pentameter (5 Iambic feet) - unrhymed is *Blank verse*. Iambic pentameter (rhymed) is known as *Heroic measure* - most frequently used of any English metre.

Grade 7

- Trisyllabic measures have not been used much by our poets - they require constant recurrence of two syllables - both unaccented - and short, to one accented syllable and our language does not afford that proportion.

- *Shakespeare* used *Blank Verse* extensively. This is unrhymed Iambic Pentameter (5 Iambic feet). *His sonnets* are composed of 14 ten syllable lines, with a rhyming pattern of:

    AB AB
    CD CD
    EF EF
    G   G

- **The Petrarchan sonnet (Italian in origin)** and the precursor of other sonnet forms has a rhyming pattern of:

    ABBA ABBA CDE CDE

- **Ballad metre** - four lines of iambic measure: (4-3-4-3) iambic feet, with a rhyming pattern such as:

    ab ab or ab cb (This is also the Common metre in hymns).

- *Eye - rhyme* - looks alike but does not sound alike:

    eight, height
    few,   sew
    cant,   can't

- *Triple rhyme*   tottering, pottering.

- Writers of verse do not slavishly adhere to metrical rules - variety relieves the monotony of a regular pattern.

- Variations such as addition or omission of syllables, the interchange of feet, the addition of a long or short measure, rhyme, all add up to the melody of the rhythm which is at a writer's disposal.

Grade 7

- *Speech faults and their correction.*

'Speak the speech, I pray you, as I pronounced it to you, trippingly on the tongue; but if you mouth it, as many of your players do, I had as lief the town crier spoke my lines.'

Hamlet, Shakespeare

'Talking and eloquence are not the same: to speak, and to speak well, are two things.'

Ben Jonson, *playwright and poet*

If the *way* in which we speak draws attention to itself rather than to *what* we have to say - then our ability to communicate successfully is impaired. Our voice is the means by which we communicate our inner self. Our aim is clear, expressive, natural speech, full of energy and vitality.

We have established that *accuracy* in speech is the result of the *correct* formation of vowels and consonants - covered in Grades 1,2 and 6 *coupled* with the *accepted pronunciation* of words. We use Standard English purely as our 'model' on which to base our work - and our aim is for speech to be an expression of our personalities, able to express our thoughts and *appropriate* to each situation we find ourselves in.

If we've studied the formation of vowel and consonant sounds in Grade 6 most of the following information will probably be redundant, but we'll go through each fault and point out why it *hinders* our ability to communicate well, and how we can correct it. Confidence comes from understanding how words are formed, how we pronounce them and how we put them to good use because:

'Words once spoken can never be recalled.'
Wentworth Dillon, *Irish poet and critic*

Grade 7

- **Substitutions**
  - One sound is substituted for another - usually *f* or *v* for *th*, therefore *th*ree becomes free, *th*under - funder. Sometimes it is due to a habit a child has adopted, as the 'th' sound can be formed and used in other words - fa*th*er. Sometimes though, a child doesn't know how to form the 'th' sound at all. How the 'th' sound is formed and its correction will be covered later in this chapter.

    also:
ch for T before oo vowel	Tuesday	becomes	Chewsday
	Tulip	becomes	chewlip
j for D before oo vowel	Duke	becomes	juke
	Dew	becomes	Jew

  - The *unvoiced* consonants, p, t, f, s, give sharpness to our speech. Voiced consonants should be properly vibrated, particularly final ones because they add resonance to the voice, b, d, l, g, z, v, th. All *final 's' sounds* after voiced consonants should be said as 'z' e.g. "sound<u>s</u>". Make sure you give each sound its full value.

  - After *unvoiced* consonants, p, k, s, f, the final 'ed' should be said as 't' e.g. laugh<u>ed</u>, look<u>ed</u>.

- **Distortions**
  Vowels are sometimes distorted from their original form - diphthongs and triphthongs are usually the ones at fault!

    e.g. 'die' for 'day'; 'toim' for 'time'.

  Often the neutral vowel hasn't been observed and therefore we over-emphasise and distort the vowel sound - 'a<u>gain</u>' instead of 'agen'; 'moun<u>tain</u>' instead of 'mounten'.

Grade 7

Very often final short 'i' sounds are distorted to EE :

party	becomes	partee,
quickly	becomes	quicklee
city	becomes	citee
pretty	becomes	prettee
electricity	becomes	electricitee

- **Omissions**
  We can give the impression of carelessness and sloppiness to our speech when consonants and syllables are dropped - rather like dirty shoes and an unkempt appearance.

  For example - we hear 'its ho<u>h</u>' for 'it's ho<u>t</u>'; 'I'm gunna' for 'I'm going to'; 'bu<u>h</u>' for 'bu<u>t</u>'; 'libry' for 'lib<u>rary</u>'; 'Febry' for 'Feb<u>ruary</u>'; 'nex top' for 'next stop'; 'din't' for 'didn't'; 'gerrof' for 'get off'.

  Speech must be appropriate to our needs - just as we have a wardrobe of clothes to match the occasion - we need to develop our speech awareness and adaptability. There is also a very important need for people to want *to fit in* with their peer group and as our lives become much more expansive than in the past, the need to blend in with any group becomes all the more apparent - it's a very primitive tribal instinct - but we also need to *develop our range* and adapt our speech tunes to the occasion, so that our language and speech is always *appropriate* to the situation.

- **Additions**
  Extra vowels are often added to words - an extra syllable is added - film becomes filum; athlete becomes a-tha-leet; trembling becomes tremberling.

  - For *film* the tongue needs to hold the L sound until the lips form the M.

Grade 7

- For *athlete* the tongue has difficulty passing from the TH to the L.

- With *trembling* the lips part too soon, before the tongue can tap the alveolar ridge and the sound blends onto the lips.

- Other examples are lovely - loverly; didn't - didunt; grievous - grievious; drowned - drownded.

- An extra g is added quite often to the composite NG sound - so that singer becomes sing-ger; singing becomes sing-ging. K is added to ng too - something becomes somethingk.

- To make the NG sound - First make sure you are lifting the tongue tip to the alveolar ridge to make the N sound, and raise the back of the tongue against the soft palate as if to make a G - allow voice to resonate in the nose.

To correct this fault - don't move tongue or jaw until the sound has faded away. The back of the tongue should be released gradually from its contact with the soft palate, or G or K will be added onto the NG sound.

- **Lateral Plosion**
  An extra syllable is often added to these words:

bottle	becomes	bott-tul
little	"	litt-tul
title	"	tie-tul
kettle	"	kett-tul
model	"	mod-dul

  Feel the tongue tip pressed firmly against the alveolar ridge for the 't' and let it stay there while the sides of the tongue are lowered to form the 'l' sound.

Grade 7

- **Nasal Plosion**
  An extra syllable is often added to these words.

button	becomes	butt-ton
garden	becomes	gard-den
pattern	becomes	patt-tern
cotton	becomes	cott-ton

  Again the tongue tip is pressed firmly against the alveolar ridge for the t or d while the back of the palate is lowered for the 'n' sound, wait until the sound is finished before releasing the tongue tip. Adding an extra syllable to both these categories sounds childish.

- **Intrusive Consonants - r, w, y.**
  Intrusive consonants may be inserted into words where they do not belong. These faults are due to a tightness in the jaw muscles which cramp the movement of the tongue from vowel position to vowel position so that the r, w, or y is glided onto the adjacent word.

  - *Intrusive r* - occurs between the two vowels in the same word or the same phrase. For example:-

    the idea of becomes the idea rof;
    drawing room becomes drawring room;
    awe inspiring becomes awe rinspiring;
    saw all become saw rall.

    To correct this fault, keep the tongue tip down below the bottom teeth when saying the two vowel sounds.

  - *Intrusive w* - occurs between two vowels in the same phrase. For example:-

    so easy becomes so weasy;
    who is becomes who wis;
    to improve becomes to wimprove.

Grade 7

To correct this fault don't let the lips come together too much before making the following vowel sound.

- ***Intrusive y***

  For example:-
  my eyes becomes my <u>y</u>eyes;
  my ears becomes my <u>y</u>ears;
  see all becomes see <u>y</u>all;
  my idea becomes my <u>y</u>idea.

  To correct this fault don't allow the 'y' sound to glide into the adjacent vowel sound.

- ***Reduplicated and Allied Consonants***
  With ***reduplicated*** consonants - the same consonant sound is repeated at the end of a word and at the beginning of the adjacent word.

  For example:

ho<u>t t</u>ea	wan<u>t t</u>o
bi<u>g g</u>irl	coul<u>d d</u>o
blac<u>k c</u>at	rip<u>e p</u>ears
fin<u>e n</u>ight	tou<u>gh f</u>ight

  The first sound is held briefly before the second sound is released. To give each sound its full value, would make your speech sound over-emphatic and formal.

  With ***allied*** consonants - the organic formation is identical - the sounds are made in the same way p, b, t, d, k, g, etc. but one sound could be voiced, one unvoiced, one sound plosive the other sustained.

Grade 7

For example:
    hot dogs   rhubarb pie
    some boys   red tie
    ten days   bad news

When trying not to sound too precise by giving each sound its full value - i.e. hot / dogs - to over-compensate and end up with ho*h* d*o*gs: hold the first ending momentarily before focusing and releasing the second sound.

- **Rebound**

  This is an *addition* of a neutral vowel after the final consonant. For example *bad*-uh. Make sure there is no release of vocalised sound after the plosive.

  For words ending with sustained voiced consonants, cars which is spoken as carz, so it doesn't become carz-uh, add an extra s after the z - carzs to prevent a neutral vowel being added. Leaves - leavez - becomes leavezs to prevent a rebound neutral vowel.

- **Faulty Junctures**

  A final consonant is attached to the initial vowel in the adjacent word:

  > 'Not at all' becomes 'noh tat tall'.
  > 'An aim' becomes 'a name'.
  > 'My ears' becomes 'my years'.
  > 'That's tough' becomes 'that stuff'.

  We need to reduce the pressure on the final consonant of the first word and raise the pitch slightly when saying the second word.

Grade 7

- **Neutral Vowel**
  Most commonly used vowel in our English Language. The fault is not observing when we use it. The neutral vowel helps make our speech flow, and we avoid a stilted syllabic stress. It always occurs in an unstressed position. (See Grade 3 notes).

- **Syllables**
  Accenting of syllables is an important feature of English pronunciation. Words of more than one syllable have a main stress (primary) and a secondary stress, or stresses. We either say the *main* stress louder or on a different pitch level, or accentuate it by lengthening it. It is incorrect to give each syllable equal weight as it destroys the rhythm of the word. It is also incorrect to stress unstressed syllables in a word.

- **Inflections**
  Repetitive speech patterns reveal more about our regional variations than distorted vowel sounds. In the North of England where I live, we have repetitive downward inflections, conjuring up images of dark, dank, depressing days. These speech patterns become habitual and are most inappropriate on bright spring mornings. Apply *thought* to your speech for more successful communication.

- **Mis-pronunciations**
  Confidence in speaking comes from knowing *how* to pronounce words. Here is a list of words where there is one unsounded consonant:

  - p - silent in pneumonia, cupboard, psychologist.
  - b - silent in limb, thumb, comb, doubt.
  - t - silent in ballet, castle, Christmas, fasten.
  - d - silent in handsome, handkerchief.
  - k - silent in knew, knife, knee.
  - g - silent in gnaw, diaphragm, sign.
  - ch- when two affricates occur together pronounce both.
    e.g. whi<u>ch</u> <u>ch</u>air, Dut<u>ch</u> <u>ch</u>eese.
  - j - also large <u>j</u>ar, Judge <u>J</u>effreys.

Grade 7

s - silent in aisle, island, debris.
h - silent in heir, honest, honour, how.
m - silent in mnemonic
l - silent in almond, calm, could, would, talk, walk.
w - silent in sword, wrap, who, whose, whole.

- **Familiar 'Sound' Faults and their Correction:**
We shall concentrate on the following sounds; 'th', 's', 'r' and the glottal stop.

Please note that the exercises used to correct these sounds are only *suggestions*. We are no longer bound by the rigid rules of the old elocutionists and there are many effective alternative methods for you to experiment with as you correct these speech faults.

- **The 'TH' Sound**
One is spoken <u>with</u> voice - 'those'.
One is spoken <u>without</u> voice - 'thick'.

To form this sound: The tip of the tongue is held *lightly* against the upper front teeth, while the sides of the tongue hold the upper side teeth. Air is forced between the tongue tip and the teeth with audible friction.

Main Faults: substituting F and V or T and D for TH.

Correction: the placing of the tongue - *lightly* against the upper front teeth is most important. The tongue should not be held tightly. It is *not* necessary to cause the tongue tip to protrude *beyond* the front teeth. Keep the teeth apart and hold the tip of the tongue *very* lightly against the upper front teeth. Blow several short sharp puffs of air over this position. Speak the following sequence of sounds lifting the tongue slowly to make the TH sound -

OO TH OO / OH TH OH / AW TH AW
AH TH AH / AY TH AY / EE TH EE

Grade 7

Glide slowly from one sound to the other and gradually build up speed.

> OO S TH S / OH S TH S / AW S TH S
> AH S TH S / AY S TH S / EE S TH S

Practice words - unvoiced TH:
thick, though, thirty, thumb, three, author, method, enthusiasm, mathematics, breathless, lengthy, bath, earth, tenth, worth

Practice words - voiced TH:
this, that, then, those, though, therefore, father, mother, weather, further, gather, bathe, smooth, with.

- ***The S Sound***
The *tip* and the *blade* of the tongue are raised to make *very light contact* with the alveolar ridge. The sides of the tongue are held against the upper side teeth. The air is forced along a narrow channel down the centre of the tongue and causes *friction*, which is audible, between the tongue and the alveolar ridge. The teeth are held very slightly apart and passage of the air over the cutting edge of the upper *front teeth* is an important feature of the sound.

'S' - Main Faults
- *TH* substitution in place of S (known as lisping).
- *Dental S* - instead of bringing the tip of the tongue in light contact with the alveolar ridge, the tip of the tongue is placed behind the upper front teeth.
- *Lateral S* - the tip of the tongue makes *firm* contact with the alveolar ridge, while the sides of the tongue are lowered allowing the air to escape laterally.
- Gaps in the front teeth influence the quality of the S sound produced.
- When there is excessive tension on the tongue, there will be an increase in the tightness of the channel. The air forced down will sound 'whistly'.

Grade 7

Correction - S is a difficult sound to make - the tip of the tongue should only make *very light* contact with the alveolar ridge. The aim should be to produce a short, sharp sound.

Repeat several T sounds; ttT ttT (soft, soft, loud) x 5. On ttT (T being emphasised) release the tongue *slowly* - maintain the breath pressure and a sound similar to S will result.

Speak the following, beginning with T, release slowly into the S and glide onto the vowel:

TSOO TSOH TSAW TSAH TSAY TSEE

Concentrate on directing the air across the cutting edge of the upper front teeth with a short, sharp sound.

Practise the following, note the lifting and dropping of the tongue to form S. Remember only *light* application of the tongue to the alveolar ridge is needed.

OO S OO / OH S OH / AW S AW
AH S AH / AY S AY / EE S EE

Compare the difference in tension between the tongue position for S compared with T.

OOST / OHST / AWST / AHST / AYST / EEST

Practice Words:

seize / cease	knees / niece	sip /zip
hiss / his	ice / eyes	loose / lose
thick / sick	thought / sought	pass / path
force / fourth	thank / sank	worse / worth

Grade 7

The English R Sound
To form this sound:
- R is usually *pronounced* before or between vowels - don't forget - sound out the word, as opposed to looking at the spelling, e.g. rabbit, take care of her.
- The tongue tip is curled back behind the gum ridge, while the side rims of the tongue contact the upper side teeth.
- It is *important* that the tongue *does not* make *contact* with the roof of the mouth.
- The teeth are held *slightly apart*. Lips are usually in a neutral position - when 'r' is sounded in isolation, but will be round if followed by a lip vowel - OO, AW.

R Sound - Main Faults
- W substitute in place of the R
- A variety of R is heard where the uvula (the fleshy extension of the soft palate hanging above the throat) vibrates against the back of the tongue with audible friction. This sound is frequently made by French and German speakers, but does not occur in our English sounds.
- R made with the teeth and lower lip - the tongue is relaxed in the mouth, the upper front teeth contact the back of the lower lip.

Exercises for the mobility and flexibility of the tongue.
- repeat several L sounds - LLL LLL x 5 (choose a variety of rhythms, put emphasis on different parts).
- SH LLL / SH LLL x 5 (*note* the curling back of the tongue to form *SH*).
- T SH SH SH / T SH SH SH x 5
- SH SH SH T T T / SH SH SH T T T x 5

Correcting on R
– Say a long, sustained SH sound followed by ER. (Keep the tongue in the position for SH as you try to say ER - the sound produced should approximate to an R sound).

Grade 7

- Repeat the above, follow ER sound with the following. Make sure that after the ER the tongue falls from behind the gum ridge to behind the lower teeth.

  SH ER OO / SH ER AW / SH ER AH / SH ER AY / SH ER EE

  Make sure you keep the tongue curled back while speaking the ER sound in this exercise.

- Using a mirror - say ER and continue to make the sound as the tongue is curled back behind the gum ridge. The tongue should be raised to show its underside in the mirror.

- Repeat - make a long ER sound and raise and lower the tongue to behind the lower teeth. The movement of the tongue should be done strongly. At no time should the tongue contact either the gum ridge or the hard palate.

- Say a long ER sound, at the same time curl the tongue behind the gum ridge. Lower the tongue sustaining the vowel ER and then form the following vowels when the tip of the tongue is behind the front teeth:

  ER R OO / ER R OH / ER R AW / ER R AH / ER R AY / ER R EE.

- SH ER then; SHRINK, SHROUD, SHREW, SHRILL, SHRED. As the R is formed feel the tongue curl a little further back in the mouth and move away from the gum ridge.

- Speak the following words, forming SH but *making no sound*. Only make the word audible when the tongue is drawn back for the R sound.

  SH RED; SH RULE; SH RISE; SH RING; SH RATE.

Grade 7

Practice Words:
Remember the *CURLING* back of the tongue - slowly at first and gradually speed up:

rich, round, rope, read, wrong, arrange, borrow, worry, thorough, serious, sorrow, lorry, dressed, break, train, shrink, fry, great, spread.

- ***The Glottal Stop***
  This sound occurs quite frequently in speech, and has no letter in spelling to represent it. The symbol used to denote this sound is (?). In forming a glottal stop, the vocal cords close together and hold that position momentarily, preventing the passage of air into the mouth. When the vocal cords part and the air is released, there is an unvoiced explosion. (A cough may be regarded as very exaggerated form of glottal stop).

  It is characteristic of certain forms of Cockney, Lancashire, Yorkshire and Scottish speech to substitute for the sounds P, T, K, (unvoiced, plosure sounds) - particularly where the sounds occur between vowels

  e.g. letter (le ? er); people (peo ? le); taking (ta ? in); neutral (neu ? tral).

  The glottal stop is evident in the *silence* between the vowel and the consonant.

- Quite often a glottal is used between vowels in single words to over-emphasise a syllable

  e.g. creation (cre ? ation); piano (pi ? ano).

- It often occurs between words where the final sound in the first word is a vowel and the word following begins with a vowel

  e.g. better off (better?off), go away (go?away).

Grade 7

- The glottal stop may occur in an attempt to avoid a linking R sound

    e.g. better_off (better?off)
    lawr_and order (law?and order)
    leisur_activities (leisure?activities)

- The glottal often occurs when a speaker gives emphasis to a word beginning with a vowel.

    e.g. that's ?awful; he's ?ignorant.

To correct a glottal stop
- Concentration should be placed on the flow of breath, rather than on the activity in the throat.

- Exercises for relaxation and breathing are very important.

Exercises
- Go through the following sequence of vowels, stressing the H sound:

    OO H OO / OH H OH / AW H AW,
    AH H AY / AY H AY / EE H EE.

- Repeat omitting the H - but leave a silence where it should occur. During the silence imagine the breath is continuing to pass over the tongue before speaking the vowel a second time.

- Speak the following words, preceding each with a silent H sound:

    H) uneven, (H) India, (H) after, (H) oozing, (H) apple, (H) awful, (H) eating, (H) elephant.

    Concentrate on imagining the sound in the *mouth* and *not* the throat.

Grade 7

- Speak the following, placing an H between each of the words:

  It's (H) uneven; His (H) apple; It's (H) awful; Stop (H) eating; An (H) elephant; To (H) India.

- Repeat the above, leaving a silence between the words, during which you imagine that the H is said.

***Exercises for Glottal Substitutions* - p, b, k.**
- In the following words, divide the words into two very distinct syllables:

  be-tter } note the sensation of raising the tongue to form
  bu-tter } the T sound.
  bi-tter }

  luck-y } raising the back of the tongue
  jo-ker } for K sounds.

  Pa-per closing the lips for p.
  su-pper
  wa-ter

- repeat the words, closing the gap between the syllable, retaining the movements of the tongue or lips for the consonant.

GRADE SEVEN WRITTEN PAPER CONTAINS ALL TOPICS COVERED IN PREVIOUS GRADES.

To summarise the main points

- *Verse pauses* - the word 'pause' has the most significance here. Effective use of silence can be as memorable as an effective use of words. A Verse pause also divides the stanzas into separate parts.

- *Suspensory* pauses - when the sense of the line is not complete - the poet has used this pause for effect, it emphasises the word at the end of the line - a partial pause, so *linger* on the emphasised word. No breath is taken.

- *Caesural* is a cutting in the line of verse *after* the word to be emphasised. Compare this with the oratorical pause for prose / drama.

- *Metrical* pause - lengthens the words in an unusually short line or silence fills the space. What effect does the poet wish to create?

- **Rhythm *and Metre* in prose and verse.**
  The sense of movement and flow communicated by the arrangement of stressed and unstressed syllables *and* the duration of the syllables (long or short) in words and phrases. In verse the pattern is regular, we can anticipate its occurrence. In prose - the beat doesn't have to be regular - remember that not all stressed syllables are of the *same* length. A writer arranges his rhythms so that they intensify the expression of what is said.

Grade 7

For prose - remember the description of sounds used in words - alliteration, assonance, repetition, onomatopoeia and other Figures of Speech used for effect. Think about long / short vowels and their effect on our ears, plosive / sustained consonants, voiced and unvoiced consonants - all contribute to the final effect.

'Good prose is like a windowpane.'
George Orwell

- *Metre* - a measured rhythm based on a two or three syllable foot. Categories based on where the stress lies:

Iambic = unstressed, stressed u━.
Trochaic ━u stress, unstressed (2 syllables).
Dactylic ━uu stress, followed by 2 unstressed.
Anapaestic uu━ 2 unstressed syllables, 1 stress
(3 syllables to a foot).

Revise Grade 3 Syllables !

'Poetry is the spontaneous overflow of powerful feelings: it takes its origin from emotion recollected in tranquillity.'
Wordsworth

- *Speech Faults*

A thorough understanding of how sounds are formed and shaped into words (covered in Grade 6) will make it much easier for you to *understand* how speech faults hinder effective communication.

*'I do not much dislike the matter, but
The manner of his speech.'*

Successful communication is based not so much on *what* you say, I'm afraid, *but* on *how* you say it!

GRADE EIGHT

Candidates are asked about:

- **Voice Production - to include an understanding of breath control, projection, resonance and modulation.**

Our voice is an expression of our personality. The confidence that comes from knowing we are able to express ourselves with ease extends into all areas of our lives. The whole physical being of the person is reflected in the voice, we communicate with each other by our posture, movements, gestures and facial expression - the *unspoken* language of the body, as well as our *tone* of voice. Our choice of vocabulary and the command we have of our language are contributory factors too. To express ourselves well in *public*, we need confidence and ability in *using* words. We therefore should *continually* question the words we use and the *accuracy* of their application.

To communicate by speech is an *integral* part of our lives, evolving out of a need for survival. Many people feel inadequate when faced with situations *outside* their familiar background of family, friends or their usual workplace.

Tension may come from feeling you are at a disadvantage because you assume you are not articulate enough, even though you realise you are capable at your work. Perhaps we feel a sense of inadequacy, because of some personal insecurity, centred around our deep rooted feelings to do with our education, class and our accent and we mistakenly believe that *what* we have to say is unimportant. How we feel about ourselves is reflected in our *tone* of voice and our stance, which in turn affects the way we breathe. Our breathing patterns *alter* according to how we *feel*! Unfortunately when you are uneasy you do not *think* clearly or *quickly* enough - and can come across as hesitant and muddled.

Grade 8

The moment you feel insecure you become *defensive*. When defensive, the body changes to a primitive 'fight or flight' response. When we are threatened the stomach muscles tighten, the muscles in the upper part of the back, neck and jaw become tense. This is the position of defence, the reaction to a situation of danger. The *physical* mechanism of the voice is *directly* tied up with the muscles. When the stomach muscles tighten, the breath cannot fill the lungs deeply and breathing becomes less controlled and shallow. Tension in the back prevents the rib cage opening out. This *tension* transfers to the shoulders and neck and limits the vocal range affecting *resonance*. Tension in the jaw restricts movement of the lips, tongue and soft palate, and our speech becomes less defined and controlled.

Therefore, in order to develop our voices effectively, we need to foster feelings of self-esteem and confidence. Our examinations provide an incentive to improve oral skills, helping you achieve self confidence in vocal expression. Confidence comes from thorough preparation and the understanding of how to *apply* your knowledge. These examinations encourage students, by providing an immediate goal and a measure of success, tapping the potential within all of us.

We need therefore to develop our understanding of the *relative values* of voice production; how our *posture* influences the way we breathe, how our *breathing* affects our ability to *project*, and controls our capacity to *resonate* and direct our voice. These in turn, influence the *way* we *use* our voice. The *catalyst* which activates this chain of events is how we actually *feel* about ourselves. What a lot of extra 'baggage' we accumulate and take on board which *directly* controls our ability to communicate!

Confidence evolves from a thorough understanding of our work, from absorbing and applying all the elements of technique. A performer who radiates a certain 'poise' in their work is obviously in control of all aspects of technique and can *relax* and enjoy *sharing* their work with the examiner / audience. This display of confidence and composure has direct bearing on

Grade 8

stance, breathing, the ability to project, to direct sounds effectively and balance the tone of our voices. These all affect the way we modulate our voices to complement the work being presented.

Our work explores two inter-dependent parallel thought-processes. We have established that we need to develop our feelings of self-awareness and self-esteem to open up our voices and reveal the inner self. *But* this feeling of self-confidence and self-assurance only comes from a thorough *understanding* and *application* of all the techniques we have learnt, throughout the Grades, and applied to our work.

Now we have reached Grade 8 we must retrace our steps through the Grades and see how all the elements of breath control, projection, resonance and modulation contribute to successful voice production.

We have demonstrated in Grade 4 that good posture is *vital* for effective voice production. Poor posture, besides reflecting a poor bodily image - 'we are what we feel' - will restrict the power of our voices. Remember we discussed mind / body unity and discovered that a positive *attitude* creates positive *energy* which is reflected in our voice. Aim for a natural alignment of the body. Check the head - neck - spine position. Shoulders relaxed, jaw free.

We adopt a developed method of breathing for speech purposes because we need to *strengthen* and *use* muscles which do not come into play in our normal day-to-day breathing. Lower chest breathing, technically known as 'the intercostal diaphragmatic' method of breathing ensures that we have a greater *capacity* of breath for inhalation and greater *control* over the outgoing breath when speaking. When breathing in, the rib cage moves upwards and outwards and the diaphragm descends - creating more *space* for our lungs to expand with air. When exhaling, we need to strengthen the abdominal muscles which contract and the diaphragm rises under control, providing the voice with

Grade 8

power (projection) and *duration* (regulating the breath supply to cope with what we need to say).

The inadequate methods - Tidal, Abdominal and Clavicular - do not call into play the *conscious, controlled* movements of the muscles needed for *projection* and *sustaining* the voice. Effective breathing ensures we have an adequate supply of oxygen to our brain to aid *clear thinking*. It also makes us feel alert and full of vitality. We need to ensure that we incorporate a breathing exercise into our everyday lives - our work must have a *physical* dimension to it, otherwise our knowledge becomes too academic and not of *practical relevance*. It would be beneficial to allot 15 minutes brisk walking per day and adopt this rhythm of deep breathing - back straight, otherwise the ribs cannot open properly, breathe *in* (from your centre); shoulders and neck free, lengthening out of your back and stomach *out;* breathe *out*, pull your stomach *in*. *Focus* the breathing on the *out* breath, sigh out and yawn! (this relaxes and opens the throat).

We understand that *breath* is the *initial impulse* to make voice but it is the *force* of this breath coupled with our ability to *direct* the sound efficiently into the cavities of the main resonators (throat and head) that is the *key* to audibility. As we depend on the *resonating* cavities for the *quality* of sound, two equally important elements are needed, we must have *space* (cavities fully *open*) and a *sounding* board (vibrating surface free) for the *amplification* of the *initial* note. We depend on the breath to start the sound, but too much makes the sound breathy and too little makes the attack glottal (put a silent H in front of the word), and the tone hard.

What do we mean by projection?
Projection is not just volume or force. Sometimes we need the *intimacy* to create a rapport with our audience, yet still need to be heard. Projection also means a *need* to *share* words. Words came about because of our physical need to express a situation. Therefore the necessity to make *sound* to convey our needs is vital. We can engage the audience through the physicality and

Grade 8

energy of language - we don't have to rely on *volume* to fill the space as too much volume loses its impact: we need sharper diction instead. Make sure you haven't developed a *habit* of stiff jaws and clenched teeth as tense and immobile facial muscles suggest a *reluctance* to share words and it is unlikely that you would be able to project your voice to its full capacity anyway.

A '*resonant*' voice means a pleasing *tone* to the ear and to achieve this we must consider how we make full use of the resonators. When we want to make sound, the breath strikes against the vocal cords in the larynx. The cords come together ('approximate') and are made to vibrate. These sound waves can then be resonated in the chest, the pharynx (the hollow space above the larynx) in the mouth and nose, the bones of the face and the hollow spaces in the head (sinuses).

As the *mouth* is the *primary resonator* we must make sure that our shoulders are not dropped forward, as the head has to be pulled back to *compensate* (for balance). This position causes the resonating space in the neck to be squashed. There would be hardly any reinforcement of the primary note before the sound entered the mouth.

We need strong *breath force* - breath is the *power* of our voice, as the sound travels into the cavities, each of which modify the sound according to the shape, size and structure of the resonator. This gives full value to each sound. The *force* of the outgoing breath contributes to the *strength* and *pitch* of the note - its height or depth.

The vocal pitch is *altered* by the *speed* at which the *vocal cords* vibrate and the size and shape of the opening (orifice). The *quicker* the vocal cords vibrate the *higher* the pitch. The *thicker* they are the *slower* they vibrate and the *deeper* the pitch - that is why a man's voice is *deeper* than a child's. Also, when we are tense or shouting, the vocal cords become tightly stretched. Shouting simply increases the vibrations of the cords and these vibrations fall on the soft non-resonant palate at the back of the

Grade 8

throat. The length of the cords affects the pitch of the voice so, the longer the cords, the lower the note.

Remember we can only *resonate* vocal / voiced sounds (all vowels and vocal consonants. We can't resonate aspirate / unvoiced consonants).

The note produced by the vibration of the vocal cords is *modified* by the hollow cavities in the neck and head. The initial note resounds and gives a 'timbre' - achieved by activating all parts of the mouth in achieving the desired *resonance* of the voice.

- **The Resonators**

    The *pharynx* (throat) lies above the larynx and extends up to the soft palate. The muscular walls help to vary its shape.

    The Mouth is the Primary resonator - it can *vary* in size and shape and so has the ability to affect the formation of vowels and the quality of *tone*. The roof of the mouth is fixed by the *rigid hard palate* at the front. The soft palate (velum) can be *raised* into an arched position or lowered to meet the back of the tongue, (where it closes the back of the mouth).

    The tongue is situated at the floor of the mouth, it is the most flexible organ of the body. Its movements greatly alter the shape of the mouth cavity. The exercises we covered in Grade 7 ensure that the Fraenum (the fold of skin beneath the tongue) is stretched. The opening of the mouth is bordered by the lips. The lip shapes contribute greatly to resonance.

    The Nose - This resonator has a fixed size and shape. The fullest *nasal resonance* occurs when the soft palate is lowered. There is some additional resonance when the voice is correctly 'placed' on the hard palate. The sound waves then penetrate the hard palate and this causes resonance in the nose.

Grade 8

The Sinuses - these are the hollow bones in the head. As sounding boards they aid *tone quality* - which only becomes apparent when the sinuses are blocked or inflamed - and the tone of the voice becomes deadened ('cold in the nose' effect).

The Chest (thorax) the sound vibrations pass along the bones which help to amplify the tone.

Good tone depends on a *balance* between the resonances in the pharynx, mouth and nose.

'Direct' the voice to *suit* the emotion - make full use of each sound.

The resonating activities reinforce whatever note we make. The more we can *use* our resonances, the easier our vocal life becomes, because we allow ourselves to cut back on effort and tension. We need to make the most of the sound possibilities we have at our disposal. Here are some exercises to help *balance* the chest, throat, head, face and nose *resonances* - as the 'well-modulated' voice is produced by *balancing* all the resonators together.

Exercises:
- *Hum*-breathe from the centre and keep the throat open. Direct the sound from the head to the nose and then the front of the face. Take the sound down to the throat and then the chest.

  To try to balance and equalise these areas, count 1 - 10. Keep the voice placed forward as you speak, use the hard palate as a sounding board. Open the jaw!

  Repeat, intoning the voice in a higher pitch than you normally speak, descending down the scale 10 - 1.

Grade 8

- This next exercise helps balance your voice:

  <u>ah</u>, ay, ee, ay, <u>ah</u>, aw, oo, aw, <u>ah</u> (9 sounds)
  add m and h; mah, etc, hah etc.

  Intone the sounds, placing them forward in one continuous sequence. First try each sound on a single breath, a mental count to 6 then repeat the whole sequence on a single breath. Remember to focus the sound forward, jaw free and remember the *power* of our voice is the breath, dependent on *posture* and *relaxation*, the key to audibility is *space* and a *sounding* board.

Tone Faults:
- ***Breathiness***
  The vocal cords are brought together too loosely - resulting in an escape of breath during speech, it is a voice quality most associated with Clavicular breathing. Growths or nodules on the vocal bands can cause this fault. Care needs to be taken that not too much breath escapes on aspirate consonants (p, t, k, s, f, th).

- ***Stridency***
  This is a *harsh* metallic quality in the tone caused by too much *tension*. Tension in the throat forces the vocal cords together and results in a harsh noise. The chin is often thrust forwards and upwards.

- ***Throaty Tone***
  An unpleasant guttural (coming from the throat) quality associated with the tone. The fault may be due to a fading of the breath control at the ends of phrases, resulting in the 'tone falling back' into the throat. There is excessive use of the pharynx. This throatiness is also accentuated by having the tongue raised incorrectly in the mouth.

Grade 8

- **Thin Tone**
  A lack of balance between the mouth and throat resonance. *Too much* of the *mouth* and not enough of the *throat* resonance.

- **Nasal Tone**
  Excessive use of nasal resonance. The control of the soft palate is slack, being partially lowered, allowing the sound to pass down the nose continuously. For all sounds except m, n, and ng - the soft palate *must* be kept raised. If there is escape of sound down the nose on *vowels* - there is a nasal effect. When nasal passages are blocked m, n, ng are heard as b, d, g. Yawn, change from ng - to ah - to exercise the soft palate.

- **Husky Tone**
  This may be a strong indication of a structural defect in the vocal mechanism. If the huskiness is spasmodic it may be due to strain resulting from excessive tension in the muscles of the throat and shallow breathing. If persistent, after a three week period seek medical advice - it could indicate the presence of nodules on the vocal cords.

We now come to the *final* element of voice production - ***modulation*** - the arrangement of all the vocal techniques of speech training in order to bring out the meaning, atmosphere and emotion of the piece you are performing or presenting - which we covered in some depth at Grade 6.

A well 'modulated' voice is one that can be adjusted and regulated to suit the subject matter. Voice can be modulated in volume, tone, pitch and inflection, and by a change of pace and the use of pause. Each element of voice production is inter-related and one element depends on the other. The process of speech is the breaking up of the voice into units of pronunciation, (syllables) which we connect to form words. Let us work back through this chain of events and consider how the varying energy levels within us colour our words. For example, if we feel elated and excited, the energy within us makes our

Grade 8

voices sound higher and our speech pace quicker and we hardly have time to pause for breath! On the other hand a feeling of despondency is reflected in our tone of voice, our breathing pattern alters, the pitch of our voice falls, we feel a need to use downward inflections to emphasise our mood, the pace of our speech is slower and our use of pause - silence- could be very effective.

Here is an extract from *King Lear*, where Lear has been thrown out by his two daughters, Goneril and Regan, and has lost everything. Unfortunately he realises his folly when it is too late. In this short speech, Lear's mood ranges from anger to despair and you need to use your vocal range and all the elements of vocal variety accordingly.

> '........................ *No, you unnatural hags,*
> *I will have such revenges on you both*
> *That all the world shall - I will do such things -*
> *What they are yet I know not; but they shall be*
> *The terrors of the earth. You think I'll weep.*
> *No, I'll not weep.*
> *I have full cause of weeping;*
>   *but this heart*
> *Shall break into a hundred thousand flaws*
> *or ere I'll weep. O Fool, I shall go mad!'*
>   **(Act 2, Scene 4)**

We need to apply all the elements of voice production we have discussed: breathing, projection, resonance and modulation to draw out all the human qualities in this emotional speech. But the final most *important* element in voice production I hope we have developed, along our journey through the techniques of speech, is to *encourage* and *inspire* our candidates to *think!*

Grade 8

'The mind of man is this world's true dimension,
And knowledge is the measure of the mind;
And as the mind in her vast comprehension
Contains more worlds than all the world can find,
So knowledge doth itself far more extend
Than all the minds of men can comprehend.'
From A Treaty of Human Learning, 1633
Greville, *poet, writer and politician*

GRADE EIGHT WRITTEN PAPER WILL INCLUDE THE TOPICS COVERED IN OTHER GRADES.

Grade 8

To summarise the main points

- We need to understand the *relative* values of voice production - how each element is inter-related and dependent on the other.

- Our breath is the *power* of our voice - the *initial* impulse to make sound. Good posture and relaxation is VITAL to good voice production, as it gives freedom to the neck and the sound can be directed to give optimum resonance.

- How we *feel* about ourselves influences the way we breathe, our stance, our willingness to communicate. Think about how we *feel* when the sun is shining, the days are long and warm, the birds sing - the air is full of *happier* sounds. Think about how this mood affects our voices, how we smile more, we walk with a spring in our step, arms swinging, we make more eye contact, we readily talk to strangers - we *feel* good and this feeling is *reflected* in our voices. Conversely, when the weather is cold and wet, the days short and dark, we move about with huddled tight shoulders, pushing the voice down into the throat. We're cold and miserable, we're almost compelled to use repetitive downward inflections which reflect the way we feel.

- Our emotional state affects the way we breathe. To *breathe effectively* we need to use the lower chest breathing method, which opens out the back and rib cage. Projection is the ability to fill the space and share our work with the audience.

- Resonance is the amplification of our initial note - we need *space* and a *sounding board*.

Grade 8

- Modulation - use of all the elements of vocal expression to colour our words to complement the subject matter. Our voices need to be flexible and used to their full advantage - so that we become a *conduit* between the writer and the audience and respect the author's intentions.

- We have explored many avenues within the broad spectrum of the Speech, Drama and Communication syllabus as we have worked through the Grades. I hope our ideas have stimulated some of your own, to create your own unique performances.

' If *I* have an apple and *you* have an apple and we exchange apples - each of us has an apple.
BUT if *I* have an *idea* and *you* have an *idea*, and we exchange *ideas* - we both have *two* ideas! '

George Bernard Shaw

CONCLUSION

- Our *aim* with the theory guidelines has been to point you in the right direction, to help *you* get the most out of *your* work and to unravel the mystery surrounding 'technique'.

- We aim to broaden your horizons and enlarge your vision and make you aware of the possibilities available to you.

- The study of Speech, Drama and Communication explores all aspects of human nature and tries to help us make sense of the purpose of our existence.

- Words are our most effective form of communication. Words create images in our minds which we recreate through the unspoken language of the body and through our voices. We need to react spontaneously to the implications that words can have - for example warm, positive words - agree, like, excitement and cold, negative words fear, dislike, disappoint. How fortunate we are, as we advance through the Grades, to commit to memory and *share* with others the words of dramatists, poets and writers who are able to stretch the imaginations of both the speaker and the listener and take us into worlds *beyond* our own imaginings. Our perspective is broadened as we realise the potential we all have inside ourselves.

- *Remember* the impact of the words when you first discovered your pieces - *remember* this response, as you strive to keep an element of spontaneity in your work.

- How do we interpret the work of a writer? How successful is the extent to which the feeling, mood and changing thought of the writer has been understood and communicated? Is our stance and the tone of voice appropriate to the piece? Did fluency and expression come from correct phrasing and emphasis? Our performances need to be relaxed and sincere achieved by complete concentration

Conclusion

- which leaves us with very little spare time to feel nervous! Our aim is to enable our students to become vocally and physically expressive - we hope our examinations prove to be both enjoyable and rewarding.

- When entering the examination room - remember you are being examined the moment you enter the room - consider the effect your body language the *way* you walk into the room and eye contact has on the examiner. *Smile* and say 'Good morning / Good afternoon'. Spend a few moments getting into the mood and atmosphere of your pieces. You may find it helpful to relate the *mood* of your pieces to a *colour*. You can think of this colour before you start to perform, this should be particularly helpful when performing contrasting pieces. Announce the title, perhaps giving a very short introduction, sound confident, positive and in control, don't adopt an *apologetic* tone to your voice. Please don't ask the examiner where you should stand, which piece do they want to hear first - realise the examiner needs to make an objective assessment and wants to know that *you are in control*! Make sure the words are really secure.

- Learn by gradual absorption, rather than by rote, then you have *time* to peel the many layers revealed in a piece. Above all, you need time to think about making the piece your own, giving it your stamp, ensuring your performance has that extra dimension. Whether performing in front of an audience or being examined, we are faced with a different situation from performing in front of a teacher, family or friends and we suddenly have to cope with nerves, an unfamiliar examiner and possibly an unfamiliar room. Please realise it is *your* examination and *your* space to work from and a *well prepared* candidate exudes a quiet inner confidence and a natural poise.

Conclusion

- By the time we get to Diploma level - all our technique should have become second nature: its usage a support to our performance. These skills are gradually learnt throughout the Grades and perfected by constant use.

BUT, if our performances and presentations still retain that vital *spark* of spontaneity when we have obviously rehearsed our pieces for many weeks, then we really have found the *key to successful communication*!

Finally, remember that the motto of the college is 'Persevere'.
I wish you every success in your endeavours!

Gillian Cohen

INDEX

Abdominal Breathing	46
Accentuation	57
Affricates	101, 103
Alexander Technique	38, 39
Allegory	108
Allied Consonants	132
Alliteration	7, 22, 109
Alveolars	102
Ambiguity	109
Analogy	109
Anapaest Metre	122, 124
Antithesis	110
Aspirate	18
Assonance	7, 109
Audibility	37
Ballad metre	126
Blank Verse	125
Breathing	35
Breathing Exercises	47
Breathing, inadequate methods of	47
Breathiness	152
Burlesque	113
Caesural Pause	117
Centred Breathing	37
Change of Thought	58
Clavicular Breathing	46
Cliché	110
Conceit	113
Consonance	110
Consonants:	98
Affricatives	101
Classication	99, 100
Definition	101
Fricatives	101
Nasals	101
Plosive	20, 101
Sustained	20, 101
Unvoiced	19
Voiced (or vocal)	18

Index

Dactyl Metre	124
Diaphragm	44
Dipthong	31, 93
Dissonance	110
Disyllabic Feet	125
Double Vowels	13
Dramatic Pause	61
Emotional Involvement	59
Emphasis	58
Epigram	113
Euphemism	113
Exhalation	44
Eye - rhyme	126
Figures of Speech	108
Foot, in prosody	118
Form	121
Free Verse	121
Fricatives	103
Frictionless Continuants	105
Gesture	67, 71
Glides	64
Glottal Stop	140
Heroic Measure	125
Husky Tone	153
Hyperbole	110
Iambic Verse	122, 124
Inflection:	55, 63
Commands and exclamations	66
Double	64
Questions	65
Simple	63
Statements	65
Intercostal Diaphragmatic Method	37
Intrusive Consonants	131
Irony	111
Larynx	11, 36
Lateral Plosion	130
Lip Vowels	14, 96
Litotes	114

Index

Malapropism	111
Metaphor	111
Metre, definition	118, 122
Metre, in prose and verse	118
Metres of Verse	122
Metrical Pause	117
Metonymy	114
Modulation	75, 153
Monophthong	31
Musicality	7
Nasal Plosion	131
Nasal Tone	153
Neutral Vowel	31
Onomatopoeia	6, 22, 111
Organs of Speech	18
Oxymoron	114
Pace	61, 69
Paradox	112
Parody	112
Pause	61, 70
Caesural	117
Dramatic	62
Emotional	70
Metrical	117
Sense	30, 61
Suspensory/suspensive	115
Verse	115
Personification	112
Petrarchan sonnet	126
Phrase, definition of	29
Phonetic Alphabet	106
Pitch	57
Plosives	18, 20
Posture	52
Power	60
Projection, definition	148
Prosody	118
Pun	112

Index

Resonance	149
Resonators, The	150
Rhythm	119
Rhythm, in prose & verse	118
Rib Reserve	45
Semi-Vowels	101
Sibilants	104
Silence	76
Simile	113
Single Vowel	12
Speaking Voice, use of	56
Speech faults & their correction	127
Addition	129
Distortion	128
Faulty junctures	133
Inflections	134
Intrusive consonants	131
Lateral plosion	130
Mis-pronunciations	134
Nasal plosion	131
Neutral vowel	134
Omission	129
Reduplicated and allied consonants	132
Rebound	133
Substitution	128
Syllables	134
Speech faults, familiar sound faults:	135
The English R Sound	138
The Glottal Stop	140
The S Sound	136
The TH Sound	135
Spondee Verse	122
Style	121
Substitution	128
Suspensory/ suspensive pauses	115
Syllable, definition of	28
Synecdoche	114

Index

Thorax, enlargement of	44
Tidal Breathing	46
Tone	66
Tone Faults	152
Breathiness	152
Stridency	152
Throaty Tone	152
Thin Tone	153
Nasal Tone	153
Husky Tone	153
Tongue Vowels	92
Tripthongs	87
Trisyllabic feet	125
Trochee Verse	122
Unvoiced Consonants	19
Verse	119
Verse, blank	123
Verse, free	121
Verse Pause	115
Voice, outline of how it works	36
Voiced Consonants	18
Vowels	85
Vowels, classification of	96
Vowel sound - what is it	10
Vowel sound - formation of	85
Vowel, single	14
Vowel, double	15
Vowels, Tongue	92
Word, definition of	27
Wormy Spaghetti, The	23

Sources Consulted

The author would like to acknowledge that the following publications have been consulted during the compilation of this book, and are highly recommended to Grade Eight and Diploma students to further their knowledge.

Berry, Cecily	*Your Voice and How To Use It Successfully.* London. Harrap Ltd 1975.
Cudden, VA	*A Dictionary of Literary Terms.* London. Penguin Books.
Luck, Gordon	*A Guide to Practical Speech Training.* London. Barrie & Jenkins 1975.
Morrison, Malcolm	*Clear Speech.* London. A&C Black 1996.
Rodenburg, Patsy	*The Right to Speak.* London. Methuen Drama 1992.
Turner, J Clifford	*Voice of Speech in the Theatre, 4th edition; edited by Malcolm Morrison.* London. A & C Black 1993.